FOREWORD TO THE
SPECIAL PRESERVATION EDITION

The 1862 Seven Days Campaign . . . While the name of this iconic Civil War campaign has almost a biblical ring to it, Christian theologians may be more comfortable assigning it to the Old Testament than the New. General George McClellan's "On to Richmond" effort was met by the newly installed General Robert E. Lee, and the result was a week of theretofore unseen bloodshed. The dust jacket of historian Clifford Dowdey's 1964 book on this campaign states that "because the whole nature of the conflict was changed by McClellan's defeat, the Seven Days was the most significant military engagement in the Civil War and one of the most momentous in American history."

And yet, in the decades following the campaign, the hallowed ground upon which these "most significant" and "most momentous" battles were fought lay, for the most part, unprotected. Some small parts of the individual battlefields were preserved, but as is the case at most Civil War sites, hundreds of acres important to telling the full story of the battles were simply never protected in any organized way. During those decades, urban growth and development from Richmond and its suburbs oozed closer and closer to these battlefields, threatening to destroy them and deny their lessons to future generations. In fact, a 1993 study commissioned by Congress selected two of the campaign's battlefields—Gaines' Mill and Malvern Hill—as among eleven sites nationwide that required the most urgent action to preserve.

In the last twenty years or so, that history of neglect has begun to change. Thanks in large part to our generous and committed members, the American Battlefield Trust has been able to save significant parts of these battlefields. At Glendale and Malvern Hill, the substantial completion of their battlefields is within reach. At Gaines' Mill, there is still much to do, but we have embarked on an ambitious multi-year campaign to preserve the most important, unprotected battlefield land in America. While it is beyond the scope of this volume, the same hallowed ground featured prominently in both the Battle of Gaines' Mill in 1862 and the Battle of Cold Harbor in 1864. Most significant and most momentous, indeed.

Books like this exceptional study of the campaign are essential to advancing our knowledge of those times, those people, and what they did. But even after reading every book on a battle, there is still nothing like being on the ground, to see what those soldiers saw, walking the wooded paths and open fields as they did, and trying to imagine what it was really like.

We are honored to partner with the University of Tennessee Press once again to make the Special Preservation Edition of this new work available to our members across America and to help save even more hallowed ground at Gaines' Mill and the other Seven Days battlefields. Please visit our website at www.battlefields.org to learn how you can help save even more of our nation's exceptional history.

With deep gratitude and appreciation,
David Duncan
President

DECISIONS OF
THE SEVEN DAYS

DECISIONS
OF THE
SEVEN DAYS

The Sixteen Critical Decisions
That Defined the Operation

Matt Spruill
Maps by Tim Kissel

COMMAND DECISIONS
IN AMERICA'S CIVIL WAR

The University of Tennessee Press / Knoxville

Library of Congress Cataloging-in-Publication Data

Names: Spruill, Matt, author. | Kissell, Tim (Cartographer), cartographer.
Title: Decisions of the Seven Days : the sixteen critical decisions that defined
the battles / Matt Spruill ; maps by Tim Kissell. Other titles: Command
decisions in America's Civil War.
Description: First edition. | Knoxville : The University of Tennessee Press, [2021] |
Series: Command decisions in America's Civil War | Includes bibliographical ref-
erences and index. | Summary: "From June 25 to July 1, 1862, Gen. Robert E. Lee's
Army of Northern Virginia engaged Maj. Gen. George B. McClellan's Army of
the Potomac in a series of battles at the end of the Peninsula Campaign that would
collectively become known as the Seven Days Battles. Beginning with the fighting
at the Battle of Beaver Dam Creek, Lee consistently maneuvered against and
attacked McClellan's Army of the Potomac as it retreated south across the Virginia
Peninsula to the James River. At the conclusion of the Battle of Malvern Hill, Lee's
second most costly battle, where McClellan's strong defensive position of infantry
and artillery repelled multiple frontal assaults by Lee's troops, the Federal army
slipped from Lee's grasp and brought the Seven Days to an end. The Seven Days
was a clear Confederate victory that drove the Union army away from the capital at
Richmond, began the ascendancy of Robert E. Lee, and commenced a change in
the war in the Eastern Theater. It set the stage for the Second Manassas Campaign
followed by the Maryland Campaign of 1862"— Provided by publisher.
Identifiers: LCCN 2020056893 (print) | LCCN 2020056894 (ebook) |
ISBN 9781621906742 (paperback) | ISBN 9781621906759 (kindle edition) |
ISBN 9781621906766 (adobe pdf)
Subjects: LCSH: Seven Days' Battles, Va., 1862. | United States—
History—Civil War, 1861–1865—Campaigns.
Classification: LCC E473.68 .S667 2021 (print) | LCC E473.68 (ebook) |
DDC 973.7/32—dc23
LC record available at https://lccn.loc.gov/2020056893
LC ebook record available at https://lccn.loc.gov/2020056894

To my sons and daughters
Matt and Janet
Lee and Nicole
Charles and Leah

CONTENTS

ILLUSTRATIONS

Figures

Maps

PREFACE

My in-depth interest in the Seven Days Battles began when my son, Matt IV, and I were researching and writing *Echoes of Thunder: A Guide to the Seven Days Battles*. I drifted away from the Seven Days as my sons Matt and Lee and I researched and wrote other critical decisions books: *Decisions at Stones River*, *Decisions at Second Manassas*, and *Decisions at Gettysburg*, revised second edition, which are part of the University of Tennessee Press's Command Decisions in America's Civil War series. Books about other battles and campaigns have been added as the series has progressed, and I have now returned to the Seven Days to contribute another installment.

The Seven Days Battles established Robert E. Lee as the commander of the Army of Northern Virginia, kept Union armies away from Richmond for two more years, had a far-reaching effect on the war in the Eastern Theater, and set the stage for the campaign that would result in Abraham Lincoln issuing the Emancipation Proclamation. Casualties from the Seven Days, along with those from the Battle of Shiloh, reasoned that the war would last longer and cost more in human lives and national treasure than anyone had thought.

These battles and maneuvers developed as a result of critical decisions. I approached this study with the critical-decision methodology, which is designed to allow someone who has an understanding of "what happened" to move to the next level and ask, "Why did it happen, or what caused it to happen?" When the critical-decision concept is understood, it can be applied to any battle or campaign in any war.

I began by asking what had caused the battles to develop as they did. Were any actions or decisions so paramount that they influenced everything that followed? This query resulted in a list of critical decisions.

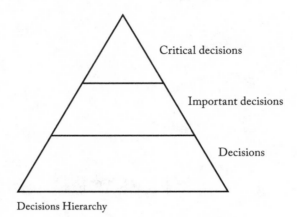

Decisions Hierarchy

This chart shows the decisions hierarchy. At the bottom are the many and various decisions, above those are a smaller number of important decisions, and at the top are the very few critical decisions. The criterion for a critical decision is that it is of such magnitude that it shaped not only the events immediately following, but also the campaign or battle from that point on. If these critical decisions had not been made, or if a different choice had been made, the sequence of events for the Seven Days would have been significantly different.

The Seven Days did not result from random chance. Events occurred as they did because of the decisions reached at all levels of command on both sides of the war. Some of these were the normal decisions made during any campaign or battle. A smaller number were important decisions. At the top of the decision hierarchy, a select number of critical decisions influenced the way the campaign and battle unfolded.

Critical decisions cover the entire spectrum of war: strategy, operations, tactics, organization, locistical, and personnel. Some decisions that initially appear to be minor are actually critical decisions that had a major impact on subsequent events. It is important that you, the reader, understand the concept of a critical decision. Without this knowledge, this book will appear to be only a short and selective narrative history of the Seven Days. Instead, this work explores the development of the battles and focuses on the "why" instead of the "what."

The sixteen critical decisions for the Seven Days Battles are grouped into four specific time periods:

Before the Battles—March 17–June 15, 1862
  McClellan Decides on a Turning Movement
  McClellan Decides on a Siege at Yorktown
  McDowell Is Diverted
  Davis Decides on Lee
  Jackson Wants to Invade
  Lee Decides on a Turning Movement

Mechanicsville and Gaines' Mill—June 26–27, 1862
  A. P. Hill Attacks
  McClellan Provides Minimal Reinforcements
  McClellan Decides to Retreat to the James River

White Oak Swamp and Glendale—June 29–30, 1862
  Lee Decides on a Pursuit
  Jackson Decides Not to Cross White Oak Swamp
  Huger Decides Not to Attack
  Magruder Is Ordered to Support Holmes

Malvern Hill and Retreat—July 1, 1862, and Beyond
  Lee Orders an Attack
  McClellan Retreats, Again
  Halleck Decides to Evacuate the Peninsula

I chose these critical decisions based on my military background, extensive experience on the ground where the Seven Days Battles took place, and close reading and research of primary and secondary material. Depending on their training and background, other historians might focus on different choices and interpret critical events in different ways. However, I firmly believe the critical decisions enumerated in this book are the core decisions of the battles. Had they not been made, the character of the fighting and the choices that followed would have been different. This change would have been of such magnitude as to alter the sequence of events from that point on.

This is not to say that Maj. Gen. George B. McClellan would have been victorious and Gen. Robert E. Lee defeated, although that might have been the case. That question is beyond the scope of this book, so I leave it to the reader to decide whether the Seven Days outcome would have been different. However, the sequence of events leading to the outcome would have changed, the orientation of the opposing forces might have been altered, the battles could have been shorter or longer than they were, and they might also have occurred at different locations.

The critical decisions are grouped into four specific time periods. Aspects of the decisions are presented and discussed generally in the following order: the situation, the options (courses of action) available to the decision-maker, the decision that was made, the results/impact of the choice, and, in some cases, other possible outcomes had another option been chosen.

One should not rule out the possibility of chance or luck, which can make seemingly good decisions under the right conditions produce adverse results. Likewise, what initially appear to be bad decisions can sometimes produce positive results. While my bias sometimes appears, I have attempted to refrain from calling a critical decision good or bad. Instead, I have concentrated on the consequences or results of each decision and discussed its effect on the campaign or battle.

This work is not another history of all of the events and decisions during the Seven Days Battles; other books provide the reader with a basic knowledge of the fighting. Nor is it my purpose to offer a new interpretive history of the Seven Days. I have concentrated on the critical decisions to lay out some basic facts and present a relatively clear outline of a very complex situation. Without neglecting important details, this account presents the reader with a coherent and manageable blueprint as to why the battles happened as they did.

As you read, you will notice the Union and the Confederacy used similar yet distinct methods to identify military units. Therefore, some explanatory comments are appropriate. Both sides identified units at the company, battalion, and regimental level in the same way. Companies were identified by a letter—A Company. Regiments were identified by a number—Fifth (or 5th) New Hampshire, Eighteenth (or 18th) Georgia. Above the regimental level, the U.S. and Confederate militaries diverged in their classification schemes.

The official designations of Union brigades, divisions, and corps were numeric and began with a capital letter. Examples include First Brigade, First Division, Second Corps or Brig. Gen. John C. Caldwell's First Brigade, Brig. Gen. Israel B. Richardson's First Division, Brig. Gen. Edwin V. Sumner's Second Corps. Many publications designate a corps with roman numerals, as in II Corps. However, this form of designation was not employed in the Civil War. The U.S. military used lowercase letters when referring to a brigade or division belonging to or commanded by an individual. See, for example, Caldwell's brigade, Richardson's division, or Sumner's corps.

Early in the war the Confederacy used a numbering and a name system for unit designations. As the conflict progressed the numbering system was used less, and the name system became most common. The Confederacy's official designations of brigades, divisions, and corps included a commander's name followed by the capitalized word Brigade, Division, Command, or Wing (later Corps)—for example, Hood's Brigade, Whiting's Division, or Jackson's Command, later to be Jackson's Corps. When referring to a brigade, division, command, or wing (corps) belonging to or commanded by an individual, the Confederate military used lowercase letters. Some examples are Brig. Gen. John B. Hood's brigade, Brig. Gen. William H. C. Whiting's division, and Maj. Gen. Thomas J. Jackson's command.

As with anything pertaining to the Civil War there are always exceptions to these naming conventions.

There is value in being in close proximity on to the location where a decision was made or carried out. Being on the ground provides the opportunity to view the terrain and the tactical situation as decision-makers did, thereby yielding valuable insights. In some cases, this is not feasible—for instance, if you are on one of the battlefields and the decision was made in Washington or another distant place. However, many critical decisions were made and carried out at or near the Seven Days battlefields. I have therefore provided an appendix with a guided tour that will place you on the ground near or at the locations where the critical decisions were made or implemented. The tour also includes excerpts from the *Official Records* or other primary source material. Some words are spelled differently today than they were in 1862— for example, *entrenchments* rather than *intrenchments*. I have left the spelling and grammar as it appears in the original documents.

Moreover, this brief guide has a specifically practical purpose: to help a reasonably well-informed reader get through the battle *on the ground* while developing further insights into the fighting and the effects of the critical decisions. This work's interpretive elements are specifically designed to support the appendix that is more like a traditional guidebook. As a whole, I hope this book form a foundation for further reading, study, and reflection on the Seven Days Battles.

Thanks to Scot Danforth, director of the University of Tennessee Press, and to his exceptional team who have guided and supported me through the writing, publication, and marketing process. Among them are Thomas Wells, Jon Boggs, Stephanie Thompson, Linsey Perry, and Tom Post. A special thanks to Elizabeth Crowder for the excellent copyediting and refining of not only this book, but all of the works in the Command Decisions in America's Civil War series. As she has since I wrote my first book almost three decades ago, my wife and best friend, Kathy, has provided constant support and encouragement as *Decisions of the Seven Days* went from concept to published volume.

INTRODUCTION

At the time of the Seven Days' Battles, America's war with itself had been going on for fifteen months. In many skirmishes and some small battles in 1861, the Union and Confederate military organizations tried to gain an early advantage and define the concept of the war. The Battle of Wilson's Creek (August 10, 1861) gave the Confederacy an opportunity to control a major part of Missouri. Victory at Rich Mountain (July 11, 1861) and Cheat Mountain (September 10–15, 1861) helped secure the western area of Virginia for the Union. Confederate victory at the Battle of First Manassas (Bull Run) on July 21, 1861, gave notice that the war would not swiftly conclude.[1]

As the war continued into 1862, a series of early Union successes gave many Northerners hope that the fighting might soon be over. At Logan's Crossroads in the Western Theater on January 19, 1862, the Union would secure large portions of eastern Kentucky. At the Battle of Pea Ridge (March 7–8, 1862), a Federal victory would secure Missouri for the remainder of the war.[2]

In the far West, a Confederate army commanded by Brig. Gen. Henry H. Sibley marched from Texas into New Mexico and then toward Colorado. Halted by a Union force at Glorieta Pass, near Santa Fe, in late March, Sibley retreated back to Texas. This ended the Confederacy's only serious attempt to expand its border on the southwestern frontier.[3]

In the Western Theater Brig. Gen. Ulysses S. Grant seized the initiative in February and with Com. Andrew Foote conducted a joint army-navy operation that captured Fort Henry and Fort Donelson. This opened the

Cumberland and Tennessee Rivers as routes of advance, supply, and communication for Union armies into Tennessee, northern Alabama, and Mississippi. Grant's victories pierced the extended Confederate defensive line in the West that stretched from the mountains in southeastern Kentucky to Columbus on the Mississippi River and pushed the rebel forward defenses back into Tennessee and northern Mississippi. In April the Confederate commander in the West, Gen. Albert S. Johnston, attacked Grant's Army of the Tennessee at Shiloh in a counteroffensive operation. Reinforced by Maj. Gen. Don Carlos Buell's Army of the Ohio, Grant fought a bloody two-day battle. The fighting on April 6 and 7 caused 23,741 casualties—21 percent of all troops engaged. Casualties at Shiloh were greater than the sum of all the casualties American armies had taken in every prior war, and these losses were also a harbinger of what was to come.

In the next two months Union forces moved on and captured Corinth, one of the critical east–west and north–south railroad junctions. Maj. Gen. John Pope seized New Madrid and Island No. 10 in April, which opened the Mississippi River almost to Memphis. Then David G. Farragut captured New Orleans, the South's largest city, and the southern portion of the Mississippi River was opened to Union navigation.[4]

In the Eastern Theater, Federal troops took Jacksonville and Saint Augustine, Florida. Then a Union force under Brig. Gen. Ambrose E. Burnside landed inside the North Carolina Outer Banks in early February. On March 9 these soldiers captured New Bern and secured a lodgment from which future operations into eastern North Carolina and southeastern Virginia could be conducted.[5]

After the Union defeat at First Manassas, Maj. Gen. George B. McClellan was transferred to the East and assumed command of all Union troops in and around Washington. He spent the fall and winter of 1861–62 creating units, reorganizing, and training his newly named Army of the Potomac. At the same time, the two Confederate armies that fought at Manassas combined into one under the command of Gen. Joseph E. Johnston. The Confederate government considered having Johnston take the initiative and cross into Maryland, but lack of troops shelved this idea. The general's army instead spent the winter months in defensive positions at Centreville.[6]

In the coming spring of 1862, Union forces in the Eastern Theater had the potential to develop war-winning strategy. McClellan's Army of the Potomac was organized, trained, and ready to be committed to an operation against the Confederate capital and the force charged with its defense. In late June other Union forces in Virginia were organized into the Army of Virginia commanded by Maj. Gen. John Pope. These troops were positioned to support McClellan's operations. Farther south, Burnside's force captured New Bern, North Carolina, on March 9 and was in position to sever some of the railroad supply and communications lines into Richmond. Concerted action by these three commands could have created situations that overwhelmed the Confederate forces defending Richmond, allowing the Federals to defeat them and capture the capital.[7]

George McClellan and others conceived of a war that would return the Union to its pre-1860 status. The social fabric of the South and the slavery question were not to be addressed. McClellan thus envisioned a limited war, but events were beginning to progress beyond that concept. In July Lincoln issued a call for three hundred thousand more troops to serve for three years. He also signed the Second Confiscation Act, which allowed for the seizure and disposal of Southern property. Even more tellingly, he commenced drafting the Emancipation Proclamation.[8]

These events and others would change the concept of the war, and both sides would start to understand that the struggle would probably be long and hard. The Battles of the Seven Days and the critical decisions that formed them would have a major influence on this shift in comprehension.

The Seven Days was a series of five battles and maneuvers commencing on June 26, 1862, with the Battle of Beaver Dam Creek and ending with the Union retreat from Malvern Hill to a lodgment at Harrison's Landing on the James River on July 2. These five battles occurred at Beaver Dam Creek (June 26), Gaines' Mill (June 27), Savage Station (June 29), Glendale (June 30), and Malvern Hill (July 1).

The Seven Days Battles resulted from Robert E. Lee's attempt to destroy McClellan's Army of the Potomac. In this endeavor Lee was unsuccessful, but McClellan's offense to capture Richmond was halted and his army driven away from the Confederate capital and across the Virginia Peninsula to the James River. Lee initiated the Seven Days with an attempted turning movement on June 26 and was constantly on the offense, while McClellan either defended or retreated.

Now, let's proceed to a detailed investigation of the critical decisions that shaped the Seven Days Battles.

CHAPTER 1

BEFORE THE BATTLES,
MARCH 17–JUNE 15, 1862

If you have bypassed the preface, please return to it and read the definition of a critical decision to fully understand the information presented in this book.

In the days and months leading up to the Seven Days' Battles, six critical decisions were made. Two of these were strategic decisions; two were operational decisions; one was a tactical decision. One was a personnel decision: if it had not been made, there would probably not have been the Seven Days' Battles.

McClellan Decides on a Turning Movement

Situation

Maj. Gen. George B. McClellan graduated second in the West Point class of 1846.[1] Assigned to the US Army Corps of Engineers, he participated in the Mexican War, was an instructor at West Point, and served in various engineering positions and as an observer in the Crimean War. In 1857 McClellan resigned his commission to become chief engineer of the Illinois Central Railroad. With the outbreak of the Civil War, he returned to the army with the rank of major general. After the Union defeat at the First Battle of Manassas (Bull Run), he was brought from what is now West Virginia to organize, train, and command the newly created Army of the Potomac in August 1861.[2]

Maj. Gen. George B. McClellan, USA.
Library of Congress.

McClellan spent the next six months organizing and training his army. Even though the main Confederate army in the East was located only twenty-five miles away at Centreville, Virginia, except for minor combat and skirmishes such as Balls Bluff (October 21) and Dranesville (December 20), there was no major operations by the Army of the Potomac.[3]

The two victorious Confederate armies at First Manassas (Brig. Gen. P. G. T. Beauregard's Army of the Potomac—not to be confused with the later Union army with same name—and Gen. Josephs E. Johnston's Army of the Shenandoah) were combined into one army. This army, commanded by Johnston, spent the winter months at Centerville.[4]

As Spring 1862, and the campaign season, approached McClellan knew he would have to commence operations with his army. McClellan incorrectly though that Johnston outnumbered him and rather than attack him directly looked for a course of action that would force Johnston out of his defense works or capture the Confederate capital, Richmond.

Options

To bring the Confederate army out of its defenses at Centreville or to maneuver to capture Richmond, McClellan had three options, all of which involved a turning movement of various lengths.

Option 1

McClellan could march overland southwest fourteen miles from Alexandria to the Occoquan River. Upon crossing the river, he and his men could then march fourteen more miles and capture Johnston's supply depot at Manassas, which was seven miles south of Centreville. Alternately, after crossing the Occoquan River, McClellan could march southwest twenty miles and take a positon across Johnston's line of supply and communication to Richmond, the Orange and Alexandria Railroad. Either of these actions would bring the Confederate army out of its defenses, and a battle of maneuver would develop. This option would focus on the Confederate army rather than the capital.

Option 2

McClellan could also use sea power and transport the Union army 138 miles down the Potomac River and Chesapeake Bay to the mouth of the Rappahannock River, then 16 miles up the river to Urbanna. From there, the Federal troops could march overland fourteen miles to West Point on the York River. Then the army could use the river port of West Point and the Richmond and York River Railroad to support the march to Richmond, 36 miles away. This course of action would place the Union army 90 miles south of the Confederates at Centreville. It would also bring Johnston out of his fortification and south to the capital. With good planning and a fast pace, the Federal army might arrive at Richmond before the Confederates.

Option 3

This option involved the longest move for McClellan's army. Again, he could use sea power to move troops 182 miles down the Potomac River and Chesapeake Bay to Fort Monroe at the tip of the Virginia Peninsula. From there, the force could march overland 75 miles to Richmond. Again, the objective would be to arrive at Richmond before the Confederate army could redeploy from Centreville, some 90 miles away.

Decision

McClellan preferred Option 2—troops traveling by water to Urbanna, then overland to Richmond. On March 7 Pres. Abraham Lincoln attended a council of war, and the next day he approved the Urbanna option. However, on March 8 and 9 Johnston's army abandoned the Centreville position and fell back thirty-six miles to locations along the Rappahannock River. This development made a landing at Urbanna unfeasible. McClellan then decided he would adopt Option 3 and transport his army by ships and boats to Fort

Monroe, then move up the Peninsula to Richmond. His plan was to arrive there before Johnston knew about his movements and could shift his army south the fifty-three miles to the Confederate capital.[5]

Results/Impact

The Army of the Potomac commenced loading on transports and sailing for Fort Monroe on March 17. John Tucker, the assistant secretary of war in charge of collecting transports and shipping troops, reported that in less than three weeks 389 ships and boats had delivered to Fort Monroe 121,500 men, 14,592 animals, 1,224 wagons and ambulances, 44 artillery batteries, and a large amount of equipment. Troops departed from Alexandria at the rate of one division per day. McClellan arrived at Fort Monroe on April 2, and two days later the Army of the Potomac began marching north toward Yorktown.[6]

McClellan's critical decision to conduct a turning movement using sea power to position his army at Fort Monroe commenced the Peninsula Campaign. This campaign completely upset the preconceived operational concept in the Eastern Theater and required the redeployment of Confederate forces from northern Virginia and other places to Richmond and the Virginia Peninsula. It was the precursor that brought on the Seven Days Battles; without it, these engagements and other events would not have occurred.

Alternate Decision/Scenario

McClellan could have decided to march overland against Johnston's supply base (Option 1). This would have brought Johnston out of his position near Centreville. Its probable that Johnston would have retreated south to the Rappahannock River, if he had not already done so. The war in Virginia would assume the aspect of an overland campaign as McClellan maneuvered and attacked and Johnston defended and delayed. Events in Virginia would have been totally different than what actually happened. If Johnston wasn't wounded Lee would not be appointed as the Confederate army commander, the Seven Days, as we know it, would not have happened, and probably not the Second Manassas and Antietam Campaigns.

McClellan Decides on a Siege at Yorktown

Situation

Maj. Gen. George B. McClellan landed at Fort Monroe on April 2, 1862. When he arrived, the Army of the Potomac had approximately fifty thousand troops ready for operations, and more were arriving every day. McClellan received reliable intelligence that the Confederates in front of him numbered from fifteen to eighteen thousand. This was the most dependable information he would have on enemy strength for the rest of the operations on the Peninsula and during the Seven Days. McClellan would have preferred to sail troops up the York River, conduct an amphibious landing above Yorktown, and secure West Point as a supply and support base. However, the guns in the Yorktown fortification and across the river at Gloucester Point controlled the river at that one-half-mile-wide passage. Therefore, he decided to move overland against the Yorktown position.[7]

The initial force confronting McClellan was Maj. Gen. John B. Magruder's Army of the Peninsula, consisting of 13,600 troops. When McClellan arrived at Fort Monroe, Magruder, born in Port Royal, Virginia, was just one month shy of his fifty-fifth birthday. The 1830 West Point graduate had been stationed in various posts in the East and West, and he had fought in the Mexican War. After resigning his commission on April 20, 1861, Magruder was appointed a brigadier general in the Confederate army on June 17, 1861, then promoted to major general on October 7. Because of his love of and expertise at conducting theatrical performances in the prewar army, he was known as "Prince John."[8]

Magruder constructed a defensive position across the Peninsula eighteen miles from Fort Monroe. The site was anchored on both flanks by fortifications on Mulberry Island on the James River and Yorktown on the York River. Between these two anchors was a fourteen-mile defensive line. Two

Maj. Gen. John B. Magruder, CSA.
National Archives.

dams were situated along this line, and three more were constructed to create flooded and swampy areas. Manning the two defensive anchors required 6,000 troops, leaving only 7,600 troops for the defensive line. With this force Magruder was ordered to slow or stop the Union advance.[9]

General Johnston received orders to bring his army, positioned along the Rappahannock River, to the Peninsula. In the meantime, Magruder had to delay McClellan until Johnston's troops arrived. Magruder used the soldiers not assigned to the anchors on the two rivers to create a deception. These troops continually moved about, showing themselves so as to give the impression of a much larger force.[10]

McClellan's plan was to advance, with the troops already disembarked, from the vicinity of Fort Monroe in two columns. The right column (Brig. Gen. Samuel P. Heintzelman's Third Corps with two infantry divisions and one regiment of cavalry) was to move directly to Yorktown. The left column (Brig. Gen. Erasmus D. Keyes's Fourth Corps with two infantry divisions and one regiment of cavalry) was to move close to the James River toward Williamsburg. If necessary, this force could turn right to outflank and cut off the Confederates at Yorktown. In the center, a fifth infantry division and the army's reserve artillery (eighteen batteries with one hundred guns) followed these two columns. Maj. Gen. Irvin McDowell's First Corps was to land across the river from Yorktown so as to neutralize the artillery at Gloucester Point, then proceed up the left (east) bank of the York River to West Point. This would outflank any Confederate positions on the lower Peninsula. McDowell's participation in the plan was canceled when President Lincoln revoked the First Corps' movement to join McClellan and retained it as a force to protect Washington.[11]

Union movement from Fort Monroe commenced on April 4 virtually unopposed. However, the next day's advance brought about changes to McClellan's tactical concepts. These changes developed as a series of events unfolded. While the roads were supposed to be good for traffic at any time, rain turned the roads to deep mud and filled the Warwick River and creeks with water. Confederate defensive positions began to show up in unexpected locations. McClellan was notified that McDowell's First Corps would not be joining him on the Peninsula.[12]

Options

Confronted with a changing tactical situation, McClellan had to decide how and where his army would maneuver. Two viable options were available to him: continue to advance with the left column, or assume a static position and capture the Confederate defenses by siege.

Option 1

McClellan and his men could continue to advance and maneuver. He had begun moving forward with two infantry columns and a reserve. Confronted with a changing situation, he could conduct reconnaissance and probe for weak points in the Confederate defenses, then adjust his tactical plans. In doing so, he would keep the initiative and force Magruder to respond to his actions. Success with this option would depend on acquiring accurate information on Confederate positions and troop locations. This course of action would also limit the time Johnston would have to reinforce Magruder. If successful, this option would maintain the momentum of the Army of the Potomac's movement toward Richmond.

Option 2

Another possibility for the Federals was assuming a static position and shifting to siege operations. McClellan was capable of this course of action, as a heavy siege train of 101 guns accompanied his army. These guns ranged from 200-pound, 100-pound, 30-pound, and 20-pound Parrotts to 4 ½-inch siege guns, 13-inch, 10-inch, and 8-inch mortars, and others. Conducting a siege would be time consuming, as positions would have to be constructed and the heavy guns emplaced. Then time would be needed to use the guns to reduce the Confederate fortifications while approach trenches were dug for the infantry. These preparations would provide additional time for Johnston to reinforce Magruder and to prepare fall back defensive positions farther up the Peninsula.[13]

Decision

McClellan decided on Option 2, siege operations. He halted his infantry's forward movement, had positions prepared, and brought the siege guns forward.

Results/Impact

McClellan incorrectly thought Johnston's army was in front of him. The forward momentum of the Army of the Potomac was halted, and he lost the tactical initiative. From April 18 to May 2, Federals constructed fourteen positions and emplaced the guns.[14]

Confederates used the time McClellan provided them to good advantage. Johnston's army commenced leaving its positions along the Rappahannock River on April 4. On April 9 Brig. Gen. Jubal A. Early's brigade and Maj. Gen. Daniel H. Hill's division joined Magruder on the lower Virginia Peninsula; others would follow. Johnston himself arrived at Yorktown on

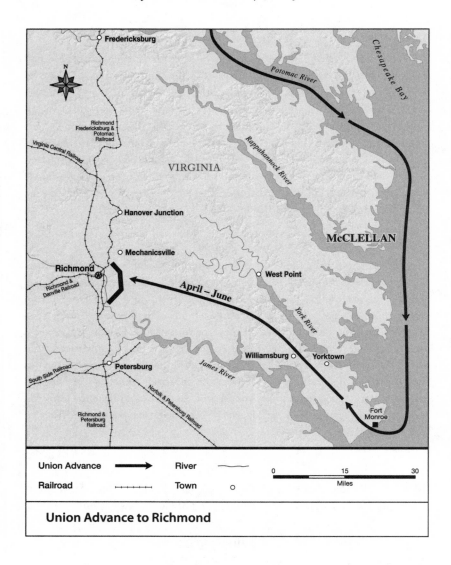

Union Advance to Richmond

April 14 and assumed command of all Confederate troops. McClellan continued to emplace his siege guns and by May 1 was ready to fire on the Confederate fortifications. However, on the night of May 3 Johnston withdrew his army from the Yorktown defenses and marched farther back up the Peninsula. In a hollow victory, Union troops occupied Yorktown.[15]

McClellan's critical decision changed the concept of his operations. He would not have an open road to Richmond, nor would he arrive there before the bulk of Johnston's army. All of the advantages of the turning movement were lost, and additional Confederate forces were brought to Richmond or positioned to support any future operations.

McDowell Is Diverted

Situation

Maj. Gen. George B. McClellan's initial offensive plan was for a turning movement using sea power to move the Army of the Potomac to Urbanna, thereby forcing Johnston's Confederate army to abandon its positions at Centreville. Before this plan could be enacted, Johnston fell back fifty miles southwest to positions along the Rapidan River. This caused McClellan to modify his turning movement, and he extended the landing area to Fort Monroe at the tip of the Peninsula. Lincoln's approval of this plan was contingent on a sufficient number of troops remaining to defend Washington. McClellan reported that he was leaving in place 55,000 troops from his army plus the Washington garrison of 18,000, for a total of 73,500 men. After McClellan departed for the Peninsula, Lincoln and his secretary of war discovered that this number was grossly incorrect—only about 26,761 troops were in position to guard the capital.[16]

Before Maj. Gen. Irvin McDowell's First Corps (33,510 troops present for duty) could be transferred to the Peninsula, by order of the president on April 4 it was detached from the Army of the Potomac and positioned to cover the southern and southwestern avenues of approach to Washington. When Johnston withdrew his army from the Rapidan River and then moved it to the Peninsula, McDowell's corps moved farther south to just across the Rappahannock River from Fredericksburg, only fifty miles from Richmond. On May 17 McDowell was ordered to march overland south and join the Army of the Potomac. McClellan's army was approaching Richmond, and the linkup with McDowell's corps would extend his position farther to the north and northwest of the Confederate defenders. Such a move would further isolate Richmond, especially from the Shenandoah Valley, and provide McClellan with a greatly increased capability to capture the Confederate capital. However, events in the Shenandoah Valley were to change everything.[17]

Maj. Gen. Thomas J. "Stonewall" Jackson began phase two of his Shenandoah Valley Campaign on May 19, when his forces again advanced north down the valley from New Market and Luray. By May 29 Jackson had driven Union forces out of the valley, and his advance elements were at Harpers Ferry. The result was to posture a threat to Maryland across the Potomac River, or a

Maj. Gen. Irvin McDowell, USA.
Library of Congress.

move toward Washington. Although Jackson did not have sufficient strength to successfully carry out either plan, Confederates in strength at Harpers Ferry caused extreme consternation in Washington. Lincoln, who had assumed command of all Union forces, now faced two divergent operational situations and had to decide what to do.[18]

Options

Lincoln had two choices for handling the operational situation once Jackson moved down the valley to Harpers Ferry. The president could allow McDowell's corps to continue moving south, or he could use it, with other commands, to trap Jackson in the lower (northern) Shenandoah Valley.

Option 1

McDowell could continue on south to link up with the Army of the Potomac. This option would significantly increase the size of the Union force maneuvering to capture Richmond. Once McDowell's corps made contact with the Army of the Potomac's right flank, the Federal lines before Richmond would be extended to the north and northwest. Troops would then be placed north of the city, further isolating it. In addition, when Lee assumed command of the Army of Northern Virginia on June 1, he began planning a turning movement around the Union right flank to threaten its supply base at White House Landing and its supply line. With a significant Northern force north of Richmond, such an action would not be practicable. Jackson's force was designed to be the key component of this offensive maneuver. However, with McDowell's corps in a positon close to and north of Richmond, the routes Jackson eventually used would be blocked, forcing him to approach Richmond from the west or to come down behind McDowell's position and initiate battle. Either way, the turning movement would not occur as Lee planned it, if it happened at all.

Option 2

Lincoln's other option was to stop McDowell's movement south and redirect his corps to the Shenandoah Valley. The president could then use this corps and other forces to attempt to cut Jackson off from the southern part of the valley. Such a maneuver would ensure the protection of Washington, if in fact that was Jackson's terrain objective, and it is doubtful that he could have accomplished that goal. If successful, such an operation would isolate Jackson from any other Confederate forces, cut his lines of supply and communication, and possibly defeat or destroy his command. However, this plan would require the effective coordination of separate, widely spaced, and independent forces: McDowell's, Frémont's, and Banks's. As of yet, this was something the Union command structure had not been able to accomplish. In addition, units from McDowell corps had a considerable distance to march (sixty-five miles straight-line distance) to enter the Shenandoah Valley at the appropriate place. Including McDowell's troops in this operation would keep

Pres. Abraham Lincoln, USA.
Library of Congress.

his force from moving on Richmond from the north and deny additional combat power to the Army of the Potomac.

Decision

On May 24 Lincoln decided to stop McDowell's movement farther south and instead ordered him to march part of his corps to the Shenandoah Valley. The objective was for McDowell to join with Frémont's command, coming from the west, at Strasburg, and with Banks's force following Jackson as he moved south. The three forces would then trap Jackson and could engage in combat designed to destroy his force or render it combat ineffective.[19]

Results/Impact

Units from McDowell's corps commenced marching for the valley on May 25. Simultaneously, Frémont's troops began their march from the southwest toward Strasburg. With an advance element on the Potomac at Harpers Ferry, Jackson realized the position his command was in and ordered a rapid withdrawal south up the valley. On June 1 Frémont's troops made contact with Confederates covering the approaches to Strasburg. As Jackson's rear guard passed through the town, this force withdrew and also marched south. Banks, who had been following Jackson, was sixteen miles behind at Winchester, and the lead element of McDowell's corps was at Front Royal, ten miles east. Jackson had escaped and would later be available for Lee to use in his planned turning movement. In a message to Lincoln, McDowell pointed out that his troops had to march too great a distance to have any effect before Jackson, marching a shorter distance, passed through Strasburg. McDowell was correct. His troops moved back and forth from Fredericksburg toward the valley and then back east. As a result, McDowell's large corps (33,510 troops) did not connect with the Army of the Potomac's right flank. Whatever effect his corps would have had on the campaign for Richmond was lost and McClellan would have an open right flank for Lee to maneuver against.[20]

After the aborted attempt to trap Jackson, the president and secretary of war concluded that it was impossible to control such widely spaced forces as were in northern and western Virginia from Washington. On June 26 (the day the Seven Days Battles began) Lincoln issued an executive order consolidating Frémont's, Banks's, and McDowell's commands into the Army of Virginia, commanded by Maj. Gen. John Pope. McDowell's corps was designated Third Corps Army of Virginia. It would not return to the Army of the Potomac until after the Second Manassas Campaign, when the Army of Virginia was dissolved and its corps absorbed by the Army of the Potomac, with McDowell's Third Corps again becoming the First Corps.[21]

Alternate Decision/Scenario

McDowell recommended that his corps not be sent to the northern Shenandoah Valley as the marching distance was too great for it to arrive in time to participate in the operation against Jackson. If this recommendation had been accepted, then his corps would remain along the Rappahannock River and would have crossed the river and moved south. In moving south McDowell's corps would connect with the right of Porter's Fifth Corps, which had been left north of the Chickahominy River for just such a connection. Such a juncture would have extended the Union lines to the north and northwest of Richmond. This would preclude the turning movement Lee planned against McClellan's right rear area, supply line, and base. It would have also blocked Jackson from joining Lee as he did in late June. There still may have been a series of battles similar to the Seven Days, but the opening fights would have been different.

Davis Decides on Lee

Situation

During the night of May 3–4, Johnston's army abandoned the Yorktown defenses and began to retreat back up the Peninsula. McClellan's troops occupied the abandoned Confederate position on the morning of May 4 and began following the retreating Confederates. At Williamsburg Johnston turned back and attacked McClellan's advance divisions. After an inconclusive one-day battle, the Confederates continued to retreat.[22]

On May 7 Union troops moved up the York River in an attempt to cut off the Confederate retreat. This effort was unsuccessful, but Federals occupied West Point and later White House Landing on the Pamunkey River, made it a supply depot, and using the Richmond and York River Railroad would support McClellan's advance on Richmond. Across the Virginia Peninsula, Union naval forces attempted to open the James River as an avenue of approach to Richmond, but on May 15 a formidable defensive position overlooking the river on Drewry's Bluff turned them back.[23]

On May 16 Johnston's forces crossed the Chickahominy River. Having retreated fifty miles, Confederate forces were now less than five miles from their capital. Six days later the Army of the Potomac closed on the Chickahominy River, and its left two corps crossed it. McClellan's army was now divided by the river.[24]

Joseph E. Johnston was born on February 3, 1807. He was a classmate of Robert E. Lee's at West Point, graduating in 1829. Before resigning his US Army commission in 1861, Johnston served in the Seminole and Mexican

Gen. Joseph E. Johnston, CSA.
Library of Congress.

Wars and was promoted as quartermaster general with a staff rank of brigadier general. He entered Confederate service as a brigadier general in May 1861. After First Manassas he was promoted to general, and he received command of what would become the Army of Northern Virginia. During the Peninsula Campaign, Johnston was wounded at Seven Pines in May 1862. For the remainder of the war he commanded the Department of the West, then replaced Braxton Bragg as commander of the Army of Tennessee until he himself was replaced by John B. Hood. After the war Johnston served in the US House of Representatives (1879–81) and was US commissioner of railroads. He died in 1891.[25]

As he had nowhere to retreat and the Union army was separated by a river, Johnston decided to attack. His plan was to bring the majority of his army against the left two Union corps on his side of the river, and it resulted in the Battle of Seven Pines (Fair Oaks) on May 31. Units that were poorly coordinated and marching on the wrong roads delayed Johnston's attack until early afternoon. Although the Confederates had some initial success, Union reinforcements eventually stabilized the defenses and brought the rebel attacks to a halt. About 7:00 p.m., as the fighting was beginning to subside, Johnston was severely wounded. His recovery would require six months. As Johnston was being removed from the field, Jefferson Davis and General Lee, traveling from Richmond, encountered him. As the second senior general in the army, Maj. Gen. Gustavus W. Smith took command of the troops that night.[26]

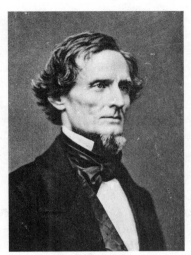

Pres. Jefferson Davis, CSA.
National Archives.

Options

With Johnston's wounding, Davis now had to decide who would permanently replace him as commander of the army defending Richmond. Davis had three options: leave Maj. Gen. Gustavus W. Smith in command, appoint Gen. Robert E. Lee to the position, or appoint a third, as yet unnamed general.

Born in 1808 in Kentucky, Jefferson Davis graduated from West Point in 1828 and served in the Black Hawk War (1832) and in Arkansas. He resigned his army commission in 1835, became a successful Mississippi plantation owner, and won a seat in the House of Representatives in 1845. After serving in the Mexican-American War as commander of the First Mississippi Volunteers, Davis was elected to the Senate, and in 1853 he was appointed secretary of war. He returned to the Senate in 1857, then resigned and returned home upon Mississippi's secession in 1861. Shortly thereafter Davis was appointed the provisional president of the Confederacy, and in February 1862 he was elected to that position, serving as the South's wartime president. He was captured and imprisoned in 1865 and released in 1867, at which point he went to Canada. Davis moved to a small estate near Biloxi, Mississippi, in 1877, and he died in 1889.[27]

Option 1

Davis could leave Smith in command. After graduating from West Point in 1842, Smith spent the next twelve years serving in the Mexican War, teaching at West Point, and constructing fortifications. He resigned his commission in 1854 to become a civil engineer, eventually serving as commissioner of streets in New York City. With the outbreak of the war, Smith joined the Confederate army and was commissioned a major general on September 19, 1861. His previous combat experience had been in the Mexican War and as a wing commander during the present campaign. At a meeting with Davis that night, Smith failed to make a good impression when questioned on his plans. Selecting Smith as commander would require his promotion to full general.[28]

Option 2

Davis could also appoint Lee to command the army. Lee graduated second in his class from West Point in 1829. Subsequently commissioned in the US Army Corps of Engineers, he spent the next seventeen years in various engineering assignments. During the Mexican War Lee served with distinction on Gen. Winfield Scott's staff. He continued with engineering duties, served as superintendent of the US Military Academy, and then was appointed the lieutenant colonel of the newly created Second Cavalry. With the outbreak of the Civil War, Lee turned down an offer to command US forces. He resigned his commission on April 20, 1861, entered Confederate service as a brigadier general, and was soon after promoted as one of five full generals.[29] Lee's first field command was in the trans-Allegheny counties of western Virginia. His campaign there was unsuccessful, and he was subsequently ordered to exam-

Maj. Gen. Gustavus W. Smith, CSA.
National Archives.

Gen. Robert E. Lee, CSA.
Library of Congress.

ine defenses on the southern Atlantic Seaboard. In March 1862 Lee returned
to Richmond and served as military advisor to Pres. Jefferson Davis, a position he held when Johnston was wounded. While Davis's advisor, he developed a close working relationship with the Confederate president.[30]

Option 3

Finally, Davis could delay his decision, consider other generals for the command, and select one of them to replace Johnston. Among the remaining full
generals there were only two candidates. Samuel Cooper, the senior full general, was the adjutant and inspector general of the Confederate army. Though
valuable as an administrator and organizer, he had no field experience. The
fifth-ranking full general, P. G. T. Beauregard, had commanded the Army
of the Mississippi for two and a half months after Albert Sidney Johnston's
death at Shiloh. In June he had placed himself on sick leave and was recover-
ing from his illness. He had also been replaced by Braxton Bragg, and he was
out of favor with Davis. Even if Beauregard was selected for the position, he
would have to travel from Alabama, where he was convalescing.[31]

Davis might also consider selecting one of the major generals in Virginia for command of the army. First among them would be Thomas J.
"Stonewall" Jackson, who was commanding and performing valuable service
in the Shenandoah Valley. If Jackson was selected, the issue would then be

Gen. Samuel Cooper, CSA.
National Archives.

Gen. P. G. T. Beauregard, CSA.
National Archives.

finding his replacement. Maj. Gen. John Magruder, who had commanded the small Army of the Peninsula until it was absorbed into Johnston's army, was another possible candidate. In the army, several major generals were beginning to show potential, among them James Longstreet, Daniel H. Hill, and Ambrose P. Hill. But none of them had commanded above the division level.

Decision

Faced with very limited options, a situation that would occur several times when selecting an army commander, Davis decided on Robert E. Lee. Lee received orders to command the Army of Northern Virginia as of June 1.

Results/Impact

Making Lee commander of the Army of Northern Virginia was one of the most consequential decisions Jefferson Davis made. It not only influenced what would happen in late June, but it also determined how the war would be fought in the Eastern Theater for the rest of the conflict.

Once Lee took command, the army discarded all thoughts of retreat or even defense in front of Richmond. Replacing the defensive-minded Johnston with the aggressive and offensive-minded Lee made an immediate impact and led directly to the Seven Days Battles. Without this decision, there would have been no Seven Days, and the course of the war in the Eastern Theater would have been drastically different.

Jackson Wants to Invade

Situation

Jackson began his Shenandoah Valley Campaign on March 23, 1862, with the Battle of Kernstown. This tactical defeat was an operational success, as it kept Union forces in the valley. Jackson retreated up the valley to Staunton and then west to McDowell, where on May 8 he defeated the Union force that withdrew west. Jackson then returned to the vicinity of New Market, joined another Confederate force at Luray, and again moved north down the valley. He was victorious on May 23 at Front Royal and then again on May 25 at Winchester. Continuing forward, his advance elements were at Harpers Ferry on the Potomac River by May 29.[32]

In front of Richmond, McClellan's Army of the Potomac had advanced to within eight miles of the capital, causing Johnston to attack at Seven Pines (Fair Oaks) on May 31. Johnston was wounded during the fighting, and Robert E. Lee took his place as the commander of the Army of Northern Virginia.[33]

Jackson, in the meantime, had sent Confederate congressman and volunteer aide Alexander R. Boteler to Richmond with a message. If his command could be increased to forty thousand troops, Jackson said he could move north, cross the Potomac River, and advance into Maryland and Pennsylvania.[34] This was not the first time such a proposal had been made. Earlier, Davis had been presented several plans for an incursion onto Northern territory in the Eastern Theater. At a conference on October 1, 1861, at Fairfax Court House, Johnston proposed such an operation, but the action was later postponed because sufficient troops were not available. Johnston again proposed moving across the Potomac River in April 1862 rather than bringing his army to the Peninsula to confront McClellan. However, Davis vetoed that suggestion as well.[35]

Concurrently with the discussion of Jackson's proposal, Lee began developing his concept of an operation against McClellan. Lee's plan would require Jackson's force to join his own at Richmond. Presented with two separate courses of action, Jefferson Davis had to make a decision.[36]

Options

If Davis sent him reinforcements, Jackson could then move north and cross into Northern territory. If Davis disapproved of his proposal, Jackson would be available to join Lee at Richmond.

Option 1:

Davis could adopt Jackson's invasion plan. This option required reinforcing Jackson with a significant number of troops. In his proposal, Jackson stated that his command needed to be brought to a strength of 40,000. He had 16,000 men; 24,000 more troops would be required. Although Lee believed Jackson's plan had merit, he thought the additional manpower would have to come from North Carolina, South Carolina, and Georgia. Brig. Gen. Alexander R. Lawton's 3,000-man brigade was formed in Georgia, and it came to Virginia and was then sent to Jackson. Lee had sent Brig. Gen. William H. C. Whiting's division of 4,500 troops to Jackson in preparation for the offense against McClellan. Maj. Gen. Benjamin Huger's division had evacuated Norfolk and come to Richmond. This 9,000-man force could be sent to Jackson as well. These forces would add 16,500 troops to Jackson's army, giving him a total strength of 32,500 and leaving him with a shortfall of 7,500. Jackson would have to execute his plan with this number of troops.[37]

As Lee wrote to Davis, the advantage of this plan was that it "could change the character of the war." The Union Army of Virginia had not yet been formed, and widely separated independent commands opposed Jackson. If these commands' performance during the Valley Campaign was any indicator, he should be able to brush them aside or defeat them separately. Although Washington was not a physical objective for Jackson, when he moved north in the valley and after he crossed the Potomac, Lincoln and Stanton would be extremely concerned about the US capital's safety. The Union officials would probably move troops from McClellan's army back to the vicinity of Washington, disrupting McClellan's operational plans on the Peninsula.

The disadvantages with this option were that it would divide Confederate strength in Virginia, force Lee to defend Richmond with a reduced strength, and prevent Lee from conducting the turning movement around McClellan's right (north) flank, as Jackson's command was a key component of that maneuver. At best, Lee might be able to attack the flank of the Union Fifth Corps in a semi-isolated position north of the Chickahominy River or conduct limited objective spoiling attacks. But for all practicable purposes his troop strength would force him into a defensive posture. This is exactly what Lee did not want, as he would be playing to McClellan's strength and ability to conduct a siege operation.

Option 2

Davis could reject Jackson's plan, leaving Jackson's force available to join Lee for the turning movement around the right of the Army of the Potomac. This choice would concentrate Confederate forces in Virginia for a single operation that would drive Union troops away from Richmond if successful.

The disadvantages of this option was that the opportunity for incursion onto Northern territory would be delayed or lost. With Confederate forces in Virginia concentrated at or close to Richmond, Union troops would have the capability to maneuver or move about central and northern Virginia at will.

Decision

This could be categorized as a joint decision between Davis and Lee. Although Davis was the ultimate decision-maker, he followed Lee's strong recommendation and decided that Jackson's plan to go north would not be approved for the immediate future and his command would be available to reinforce Lee.

Results/Impact

Davis's choice of Option 2 precluded an attempted incursion into Union territory in the late spring of 1862. Davis, Lee, and Jackson did not forget the concept, but it would require driving the Army of the Potomac away from Richmond and defeating the newly created Army of Virginia at Second Manassas before it could become an operational reality.

Jackson's Command, reinforced with Whiting's Division and Lawton's Brigade—7,500 troops—was now available for Lee to add to the planned turning movement around McClellan's right (north) flank. Jackson's 23,500 troops would be a major component of Lee's maneuver; in fact, without Jackson such a maneuver probably would not have been feasible, and it would have forced Lee's to launch a limited offensive operation or remain on the defense. Had this happened there would have been no Seven Days Battles, and history would have recorded some other series of events in June 1862.

Lee Decides on a Turning Movement

Situation

After the Battle of Seven Pines (Fair Oaks) and Lee's assumption of command, the Army of Northern Virginia withdrew closer to Richmond.[38] The Confederate position ran north from Chaffin's Bluff on the James River, crossed the River Road four miles from Richmond, then in succession crossed the Darby Town, Charles City, Williamsburg, and Nine Mile Roads about five miles east of the capital to a point on the Chickahominy River a little above New Bridge. The position then continued up the river to Meadow Bridge. The defenses were occupied by six divisions, with Longstreet's situated on the right. Next to Longstreet's men and in order from right to left (south to north) were Huger's, D. H. Hill's, Magruder's, and Whiting's Divisions , and A. P. Hill's Division formed the left.[39]

The Army of the Potomac followed and assumed positions that would allow McClellan to conduct a siege of the Confederate forces defending Richmond. The majority of the army, the Second, Third, Fourth, and Six Corps, was south of the Chickahominy River. However, as Maj. Gen. Irvin McDowell's corps was stationed at Fredericksburg, its men were expected to march south and join McClellan on the right (north) flank. The Fifth Corps' three divisions were positioned north of the river to facilitate this junction and extension of the Union position. But because of Jackson's operations in the Shenandoah Valley, McDowell's move south was canceled. White House Landing became McClellan's supply base. The Union army required 500 tons of food and forage and 100 tons of material daily. The Richmond and York River Railroad was McClellan's main supply line. The railroad proceeded west eleven miles from White House Landing, crossed the Chickahominy River, and then proceeded three miles to Savage Station and another seven miles to Richmond. Along this railroad at Savage, Forage, Orchard, and Fair Oaks Stations a large amount of supplies were stockpiled where division, brigade and regimental supply and ordnance officer could have requisitions fill and transported by wagons to the troops. The railroad was also necessary for moving the heavy siege guns from the supply base to the firing positions near Richmond.[40]

Within five days of assuming command of the army, Lee wrote to Davis that McClellan would conduct a siege to reduce the Confederate defenses and capture Richmond. Lee realized that he would have to do something other than wait on McClellan's actions.[41] In mid-June, Lee ordered Brig. Gen. J. E. B. Stuart to conduct a reconnaissance of the area north of the Union right flank. Stuart not only did so but also rode across the Union rear area and the area next to the Union left flank on his return to Richmond. This reconnaissance found that the Union position did not extend beyond Beaver Dam Creek. The most important information Stuart obtained was that no Union fortifications stood on the ridge between the headwaters of Beaver Dam Creek, a tributary of the Chickahominy and Pamunkey Rivers. This high ground formed the watershed of the rivers. A road along this ridge could

Brig. Gen. J. E. B. Stuart, CSA.
Library of Congress.

provide an avenue of approach into the Union rear area and allow Confederates to threaten or even cut McClellan's supply line.[42]

Options

Facing a large Union army just outside of Richmond that was preparing to conduct siege operations, Lee had four courses of action available to him: remain on the defense, conduct a turning movement around the Union north (right) flank, conduct a turning movement around the Union south (left) flank, or launch a frontal attack.

Option 1

Lee's army could remain in its defensive position just outside of Richmond. Confederates could strengthen the position by constructing trenches and earthworks from which to fight and erecting barriers and obstacles to slow any attacking Union force. In addition, more troops could eventually be brought in to reinforce Lee's army. A defense would force McClellan to conduct a siege operation, which he was already planning, or a frontal attack. This development might provide Lee with the opportunity to conduct counterattacks or spoiling attacks against the Union troops. An unsuccessful and prolonged siege might make McClellan maneuver left or right around the Confederates, giving Lee the chance to shift to a battle of maneuver.

However, McClellan would maintain the tactical initiative, and Lee would respond to his actions.

Option 2

Lee could conduct a turning movement around the Union north (right) flank. This offensive maneuver would avoid directly attacking the Federal forces in front of Richmond, but it would require the shifting of significant numbers of troops to the Confederate left flank. If successful, this course of action would force McClellan to reorient his army from facing Richmond to the north to protect his line of supply and supply base at White House Landing. Doing so would bring McClellan out of his prepared positions and redirect both armies' operations from a siege and defense to maneuver warfare. Initially, Lee would only have to contend with the Union Fifth Corps north of the Chickahominy River. In addition, he would gain the tactical initiative and occupy a location with considerable maneuver space.

Option 3

Alternatively, the Confederates could launch a turning movement around the Union south (left) flank. As in Option 2, this offensive maneuver would avoid directly attacking the Union forces in front of Richmond. It would also require shifting significant numbers of troops to the Confederate right flank. While a turning movement around the Federal left would not immediately threaten McClellan's supply line and supply base, it would eventually do so. This move would bring the rebels to a position from which they could threaten the enemy's left flank and potentially conduct operations in its rear area. McClellan would then be forced to redeploy from his siege positions and face Lee in maneuver warfare. The majority of the Army of the Potomac, four corps, was stationed south of the Chickahominy River, and maneuver space was more restricted in this plan than in Option 2. However, a turning movement on the Union left would give Lee the tactical initiative.

Option 4

Finally, Lee could carry out a frontal attack. This type of offensive maneuver could possibly be the costliest in terms of casualties. The attacking force should usually have more manpower than the defenders, at least at the point of contact. However, this was a ratio that Lee could not achieve. Although the rebel commander would gain the tactical initiative, the cost of doing so would probably be prohibitive.

Dabbs House, Lee's headquarters. Author.

Decision

Lee decided to conduct a turning movement around McClellan's north (right) flank. Stuart's reconnaissance on June 12–15 provided information concerning the terrain, roads, and position of Union troops north of the Chickahominy River that assisted in Lee's decision. The location of McClellan's supply base and line of supply was another important factor in this choice.

Results/Impact

In preparation for the turning movement, Lee repositioned the divisions of his army. Huger's Division was placed astride the Charles City Road extending toward the Darbytown Road on the right (south) and the Williamsburg Road on the left (north). Magruder's command, consisting of D. R. Jones's, McLaws's, and Magruder's Divisions, connected with Huger's left and extended across New Bridge toward Mechanicsville. The left of the line connected with A. P. Hill's Division, which covered the Chickahominy River from the Mechanicsville Road north to Meadow Bridge. Branch's Brigade of A. P. Hill's Division was farther north at Half Sink. D. H. Hill's and Longstreet's Divisions were on the same wing, but they did not occupy the lines. Maj. Gen. Theophilus H. Holmes's division had arrived from North Carolina, and it was camped south of the James River and prepared to cross and join Lee. As part of a deception plan, Lee had sent Whiting's Division toward the Shenandoah Valley as if Jackson were being reinforce for another

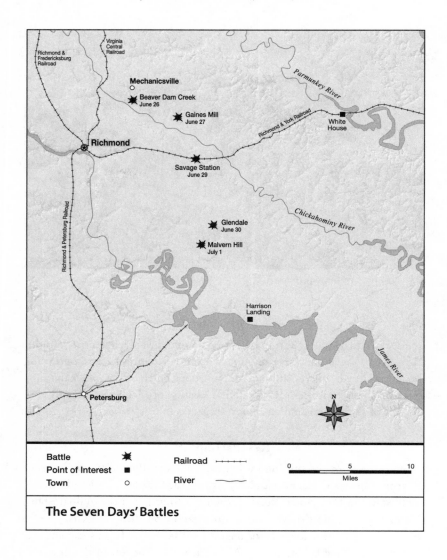

The Seven Days' Battles

operation down the valley. Jackson was ordered from the valley to join Lee for the attack on McClellan, and Whiting's Division joined Jackson at Hanover Junction.[43]

Prior to receiving orders to join Lee, Jackson had proposed that his command be reinforced to a strength of forty thousand. With this force he would move north down Shenandoah Valley, destroy the Union force near Winchester, then cross the Potomac River at Williams Port and march into Maryland and Pennsylvania. Believing the first priority was to defeat McClellan, Lee ordered Jackson to join him instead. It is interesting to note that when Lee was considering what to do after the Battle of Second Manassas, Jackson also proposed a move to the northern part of the valley and then into Maryland and Pennsylvania.[44]

Lee's operation order called for Jackson to move down from Ashland and head for Old Cold Harbor. A. P. Hill was to cross the Chickahominy at Meadows Bridge as soon as Jackson was near, drive the Union troops away from Mechanicsville, and move toward Old Cold Harbor. Without being seen, Longstreet and then D. H. Hill were to move their divisions as close as they could to the Mechanicsville Bridge. They would subsequently cross the Chickahominy River at Mechanicsville to support A. P. Hill and Jackson. Magruder's Command and Huger's Division would hold positions in front of Richmond and conduct demonstrations and feints to keep the large remainder of the Army of the Potomac in place.[45]

If Lee's turning movement was successful, McClellan's railroad supply line would be threatened and possibly severed. This would bring the Union corps south of the Chickahominy River out of their siege positions to either retreat or give battle.[46]

The commencement of this operation began the Seven Days Battles. Lee's plan completely changed the war in Virginia. The Confederate army commander took the initiative from McClellan, drove his army away from Richmond, and ended the Peninsula Campaign. Lee's troops eventually made McClellan's army evacuate the Virginia Peninsula, setting the stage for shifting the center of the war in the East back to northern Virginia, and ultimately setting the stage for the Maryland Campaign, Lee's first incursion into Union territory.

CHAPTER 2

MECHANICSVILLE AND GAINES' MILL, JUNE 26–27, 1862

During this time period three critical decisions were made. These choices initiated the Seven Days Battles, though not as planned; limited Union forces north of the Chickahominy River, which gave up a Union advantage with good defensible terrain; and moved the conflict south toward the James River.

A. P. Hill Attacks

Situation

After the Battle of Seven Pines (Fair Oaks), the Confederate army withdrew to positions just outside of Richmond. McClellan's Army of the Potomac followed and by mid-June was preparing to begin siege operations. McClellan's supply base was established at White House Landing, and the Richmond and York River Railroad was being used to forward supplies and the heavy siege guns. The army deployed one corps (the Fifth) north of the Chickahominy River and four corps south of the river.[1]

Lee realized that McClellan was preparing to conduct a siege operation, what he called a "battle of post from position to position undercover of heavy guns," to capture Richmond. The Confederate commander also knew that he had insufficient forces to defeat McClellan's siege. Lee's first move was to create defensive positions that a minimum force could occupy, thereby freeing troops that could be concentrated for an offensive maneuver. On June 3 he instructed Maj. Walter H. Stevens, the army's chief engineer, to examine the terrain to determine the best position to fight a battle or resist an enemy advance. Lee wanted positions along this line prepared for field guns and infantry. He then ordered each division to furnish three hundred men as work parties to construct earthworks, rifle pits, and lines of abatis.[2]

Lee decided to conduct a turning movement around McClellan's north (right) flank; the purpose was to threaten McClellan's supply base at White House Landing and his supply line and to insert a large Confederate force in the Union rear area. These threats would force McClellan to leave his entrenchments and engage in a battle of maneuver. In the afternoon of June 23, at the Dabbs House—his headquarters—Lee issued the order for the forthcoming operation. Magruder's three divisions and Huger's Division would occupy the defensive works in front of McClellan. A. P. Hill's, D. H. Hill's, and Longstreet's Divisions with Jackson's Command would be the maneuver force.

Jackson would come from the Shenandoah Valley. He was to march southeast from Ashland to Hundley's Corner and then to the Mechanicsville Turnpike, which would place him in McClellan's right rear. A. P. Hill's Division, the left of the army position at Richmond, was to occupy terrain near Mechanicsville. Upon learning that Jackson was at Hundley's Corner, to cross the Chickahominy River at Meadow Bridge, and drive Union forces away from Mechanicsville. This action, in turn, would allow D. H. Hill's and then Longstreet's Divisions to cross the river at the bridge on the Mechanicsville Turnpike. A. P. Hill's, D. H. Hill's, and Longstreet's troops would then sweep down the Chickahominy River. In the meantime, Jackson was to maneuver toward Old Cold Harbor. This movement would force McClellan to reorient his army to defend his supply base and supply line, bringing Union forces from the Richmond siege positions out onto open ground and commencing a battle of maneuver.[3]

Ambrose Powell Hill was thirty-six years old at time of the Seven Days Battles. After graduating from West Point in 1847, he saw service in Mexico and against the Seminoles. With the outbreak of the Civil War, he resigned his US Army commission and entered Confederate service as a colonel. He earned promotion to brigadier general in February 1862 and participated in the Peninsular Campaign. Promoted to major general in May 1862, he then commanded a division in the Seven Days. After his promotion to lieutenant general in May 1863, Hill commanded a newly organized corps. He participated in every battle of the Army of Northern Virginia until he was killed in action on April 2, 1865.[4]

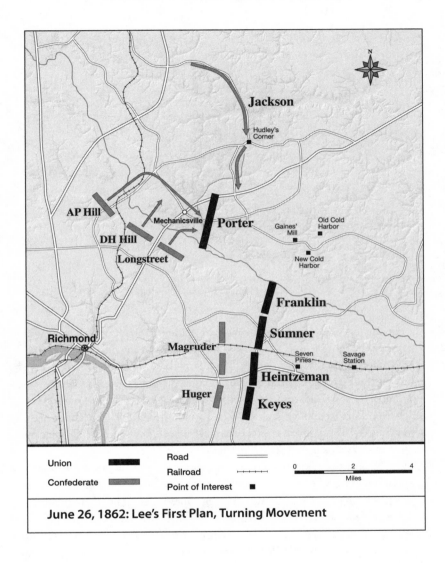

June 26, 1862: Lee's First Plan, Turning Movement

The key piece in Lee's plan was Jackson's Command, consisting of three divisions with about 23,500 troops. Jackson's mission was to reach a position from which he could maneuver into the right rear of the Union army, force it to come out of its positions in front of Richmond, and fight a battle of maneuver. The operations order gave June 26, at Jackson's selection, as the day to launch this turning movement. To meet this schedule, Jackson had to be in position at Hundley's Corner by the night of June 25.[5]

Maj. Gen. Ambrose Powell Hill, CSA.
U. S. Army Heritage Education Center.

Having just completed the Shenandoah Valley Campaign, Jackson was at Port Republic in mid-June. On June 18 he commenced moving his command eastward through the Blue Ridge Mountains pass at Waynesboro, where trains on the Virginia Central Railroad shuttled troops through Charlottesville and Gordonsville, and then on to Frederick's Hall (about eighty-five miles from Port Republic). Jackson called a halt at Frederick's Point because it was Sunday. The railroad tracks beyond had been destroyed by Union cavalry, so rebel troops proceeded from that point on foot.[6]

On June 23 the eastward movement continued, and by June 25 Jackson's command had marched thirty-two miles to the vicinity of Ashland. Thus, on June 25 Jackson's force was about twelve or more miles from where it should have been. Troops recommenced marching in the early hours of June 26, the day designated for Lee's operation to begin. The command required almost the entire day to reach Hundley's Corner, from which it could maneuver into the Union right rear and accomplish a turning movement. However, on that day it was too late to do so.[7]

The signal for A. P. Hill to cross the Chickahominy River and initiate the rest of the army's movements would come from Brig. Gen. Lawrence O'B. Branch, whose brigade was positioned at Half Sink, about seven miles north of A. P. Hill's left flank. When Branch made contact with Jackson's marching column, he would inform A. P. Hill, who would then order his division across the Chickahominy River. However, Jackson was considerably behind

Lee, D. H. Hill, and Longstreet at Chickahominy Bluffs waiting for the attack to commence. National Park Service.

schedule. He had communicated this fact to Branch, but the information had not been passed on to A. P. Hill or Lee, who was two miles south on the Mechanicsville Turnpike with D. H. Hill and Longstreet. Lee had not sent a staff officer or a courier to A. P. Hill to inquire about the delay. Nor had A. P. Hill sent a staff officer or courier to Branch ask about the postponement. In this information vacuum, the time was approaching when a decision would be needed.

Options

As the day progressed into midafternoon, A. P. Hill faced a decision. Understanding the key role his division played, he could continue to remain in position until he heard from Branch, or he could order his division across the river in an attack.

Option 1

A. P. Hill could remain in his attack position until Branch notified him of Jackson's arrival. Lee's plan was predicated on Jackson's force maneuvering into the right rear area of the Army of the Potomac. This turning movement would bring the Army of the Potomac out of its siege positions and onto open terrain, where a battle of maneuver could be conducted. This option would also conform to Lee's plan, concentrating the combat power of Jackson's force and A. P. Hill's, D. H. Hill's and Longstreet's Divisions in the turning movement and against the three divisions of the Fifth Corps, north of the Chickahominy River.

However, A. P. Hill began to consider his options at midafternoon. Sunset was at 7:36 p.m., and it would be dark thirty minutes later. If Jackson did not reach his attack positions soon, his men might not have sufficient daylight to carry out Lee's plan. In this case, Lee would have to extend the initiation of the turning movement to the following morning. Sufficient evidence shows that McClellan probably knew a Confederate force was approaching from the north. Given time, he could reinforce and reposition the Fifth Corps, or he could withdraw it south of the Chickahominy, thereby altering the Union troop deployment that Lee's plan was based on. Alternatively, discovering what Lee was doing, McClellan might order his four corps south of the river to attack the limited defenses in front of them, a choice that would probably lead to the capture of Richmond.[8]

Option 2

A. P. Hill could order his division to cross the Chickahominy River and attack. By sending his men across the river at Meadow Bridge and then toward Mechanicsville, Hill would open the bridge crossing for D. H. Hill and Longstreet. Selecting this option would initiate with A. P. Hill's, D. H. Hill's and Longstreet's Divisions part of the battle that Lee had planned for June 26. Neither A. P. Hill nor Lee knew the location of Jackson's Command. Therefore, A. P. Hill would not know whether Jackson was close enough to initiate the turning movement Lee planned. If Jackson was not close, then the offense would only have about 50 percent of its projected strength. However, if A. P. Hill did not initiate combat actions that afternoon, the offense would be postponed until the next day, providing McClellan and Porter the time to reinforce and reposition part of the defenses north of the Chickahominy. They might even withdraw to terrain closer to or on the south side of the river.

Decision

Maj. Gen. A. P. Hill decided that he would initiate the operation and ordered his division to cross the Chickahominy River and move toward Mechanicsville. He did so without consulting Lee or even informing the army commander of his actions.

Results/Impact

At 3:00 p.m. on June 26, A. P. Hill's Division began crossing the Chickahominy River at Meadow Bridge, then turned in an easterly direction and

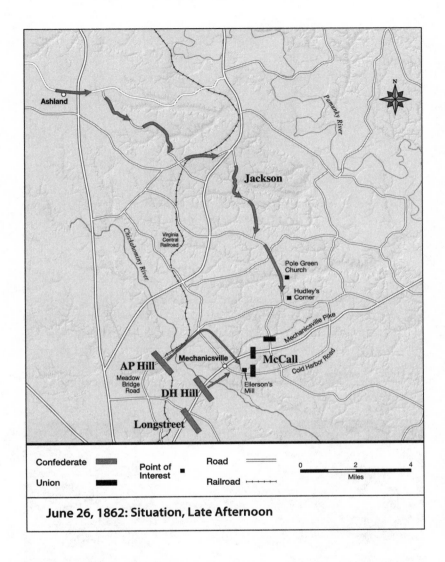

June 26, 1862: Situation, Late Afternoon

moved toward Mechanicsville while driving in Union skirmishers. Just beyond Mechanicsville the Confederates encountered a strong Union position. Brig. Gen. Fitz John Porter had deployed his Fifth Corps with Brig. Gen. George A. McCall's Third Division (the Pennsylvania Reserves) along Beaver Dam Creek, Brig. Gen. George W. Morell's First Division behind in a supporting position, and a brigade positioned to protect the corps' right (north) flank. Brig. Gen. George Sykes's Second Division was stationed farther back.[9]

Brig. Gen. Fitz John Porter, USA.
Library of Congress.

Born in 1822, Fitz John Porter was thirty-nine years old when the Seven Days Battles occurred. He had graduated from the US Military Academy in 1845, fought in the Mexican War, taught at West Point, and then served as Albert Sidney Johnston's adjutant in the Utah Expedition. After the war's outbreak, Porter was promoted to brigadier general of volunteers in August 1861. He joined McClellan in Washington to help train the new troops of the

Modern bridge and Cold Harbor Road crossing Beaver Dam Creek. Author.

Army of the Potomac. During the Peninsula Campaign Porter commanded a division, then the Fifth Corps, and rose to the rank of major general. After the Seven Days his corps was attached to Maj. Gen John Pope's Army of Virginia, and his troops subsequently fought in the Second Battle of Manassas.[10]

Pope brought charges of disobedience and misconduct against Porter after the Battle of Second Manassas. Following the Maryland Campaign, Porter was relieved of command, court-martialed, found guilty, and dismissed from the army. In 1879 a board of officers exonerated Porter, but it was not until 1886 that President Cleveland returned him to the army's officer rolls with the rank of colonel. Porter died in 1901.[11]

A. P. Hill's Division deployed and attacked Porter's position on the east side of Beaver Dam Creek. As he could see and hear A. P. Hill's advance, Lee incorrectly assumed the division had made a connection with Jackson. As the attack developed, Longstreet's and D. H. Hill's Divisions received orders to cross the river. D. H. Hill's leading brigade, Brig. Gen. Roswell S. Ripley's, was thrown into the fight to support A. P. Hill, and the unit attacked the Union Beaver Dam Creek defenses. When Lee realized that A. P. Hill had attacked on his own, he decided things had gone so far that the assaults had to continue. All of the Confederate attacks were unsuccessful, with many units suffering high casualties. During the night and early the next morning, the Union troops abandoned this position and moved back to a new one on the high ground overlooking Boatswain's Creek.[12]

Historic Old Cold Harbor Road. Author.

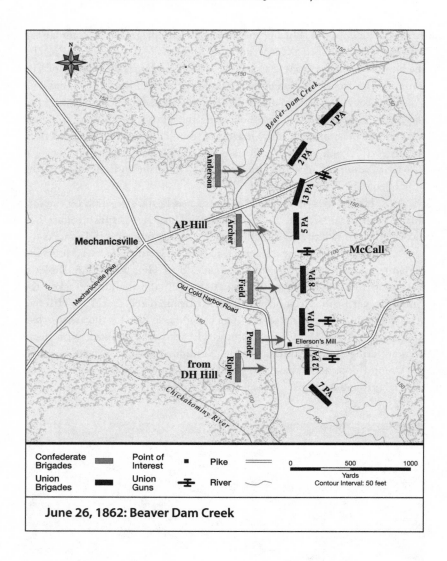

June 26, 1862: Beaver Dam Creek

A. P. Hill's attack began the Seven Days Battles. Hill launched the assault without Jackson's troops, and his men were repulsed with significant casualties. Not all Confederate forces had crossed the Chickahominy, and it was possible for Porter to counterattack and destroy or severely damage A. P. Hill's and Ripley's Brigades before the remainder of D. H. Hill's and Longstreet's Divisions could cross the river. If Porter counterattacked, repositioning Sykes's division and reinforcements from south of the river could protect his right flank from Jackson's force. Although Porter's Fifth Corps was in a good position and could easily be reinforced, McClellan began a pattern in which he would order a retreat no matter how successful his troops had been. This pattern would define the Seven Days Battles for the Army of the Potomac.

McClellan Provides Minimal Reinforcements

Situation

McClellan order Porter to retreat from Beaver Dam Creek. On the night of June 26 and the early morning of June 27 Porter's Fifth Corps fell back four miles to a new location overlooking Boatswain's Swamp and Creek. When the troops finished withdrawing, Porter's corps occupied a position on a plateau elevated forty to eighty feet above the swamp. The position formed an arc with Brig. Gen. George Morell's three-brigade division facing west and northwest and Brig. Gen. George Sykes's three-brigade division, on Morell's right, facing north. McCall's three-brigade division initially was in reserve. Porter had seventeen artillery batteries with ninety-six guns, and the defenders numbered about twenty-seven thousand troops. South of the Chickahominy River, the Sixth Corps' three batteries of long-range guns could fire into any Confederates attacking the west-facing Union defenders. Porter's position guarded four military-constructed bridges crossing the Chickahominy River. The bridges

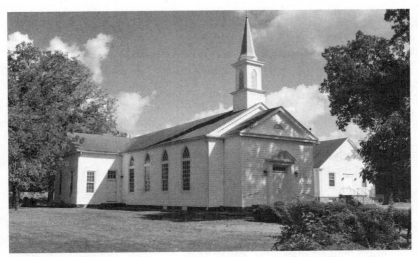

Walnut Grove Church. Author.

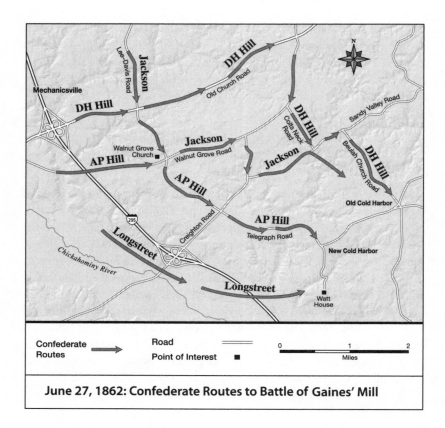

June 27, 1862: Confederate Routes to Battle of Gaines' Mill

provided routes for reinforcements to reach his men and, if necessary, routes of retreat for the soldiers.[13]

After Porter's withdrawal from his position of June 26, Lee assumed the Union Fifth Corps would occupy a position just over three miles to the east along Powhite (pronounce Po-hite) Creek. Boatswain's Swamp and Creek were not on Lee's map. The rebel commander planned for another turning movement. Longstreet's and A. P. Hill's Divisions would apply frontal pressure on the defenders while D. H. Hill's Division and Jackson's Command performed the turning movement into the area behind Porter's right flank.[14]

Longstreet and A. P. Hill reached Powhite Creek, discovered Porter was not there, and then continued on until they made contact with the defenders facing west and northwest at Boatswain's Swamp. D. H. Hill and Jackson reached a position that they thought was in Porter's rear area, but it in fact ran into north-facing Union defenders. With this situation, Lee decided to attack with all of his fifty-five thousand troops.[15]

Options

With Lee committing a large part of his force to attack Porter's defensive position, McClellan had to determine his response. The Union army commander had four options to select from: provide Porter significant reinforcements, send reinforcing troops to attack Lee's left (east) flank, provide minimal reinforcements, or attack the Richmond defenses.

Option 1

Porter's corps occupied a strong defensive position overlooking Boatswain's Swamp. However, for an extended successful defense he would need additional combat power. McClellan could make Porter's defense the deciding battle by sending a significant number of troops across the Chickahominy River to reinforce him. This option might allow Porter to defeat Lee's frontal attacks. Such a defeat would have detrimental consequences for Lee that day and possibly in the future.

Option 2

While Porter's corps was holding Lee in position, McClellan could send a significant force across the river to attack Lee's left (east) flank, which consisted of D. H. Hill's Division. This flank was exposed, as it was not anchored on any terrain feature or river, and the terrain was favorable for maneuver. Such a counterattack could result in extensive damage to D. H. Hill's Division and other divisions to his right. It could also disrupt Lee's attack and possibly make him fall back and reassess his plans. This option in combination with Option 1 might provide a significant Union victory, regain the initiative for the Federals, and lead to a direct attack or continued siege against Richmond.

Option 3

McClellan could provide Porter minimum reinforcement to assist in his defense. With the strength of Lee's force once it was totally committed to an attack, this option would only postpone the inevitable. Confederates would eventually destroy Porter's corps or drive its troops off their position and into a retreat south of the Chickahominy River.

Option 4

While Porter occupied a significant amount of the Confederate army, McClellan could attack through the weakly held defenses to capture Richmond. If selected, such a choice would invalidate all that Lee had done to protect the Confederate capital. As McClellan's position provided an interior

Watt House, Porter's headquarters. Author.

line, he could probably accomplish this assault before Lee could send reinforcements back to Richmond.

Decision

McClellan decided that he would only reinforce Porter with a minimum number of troops, and he hesitated to take even this action. This was the decision of a commander thinking solely of defense and possible retreat rather than going on the offense and regaining the initiative.

Results/Impact

Porter's Fifth Corps conducted a defense against a growing Confederate force throughout the afternoon of June 27. The combat began with the arrival of A. P. Hill's Division, later supported by Longstreet's Division; these units would become the Confederate right. D. H. Hill's Division subsequently arrived on what would become the Confederate left. Jackson's Command filled in the gap between the left and the right.[16]

There was no corresponding buildup of the defending force. In the afternoon Brig. Gen. Henry W. Slocum's division was ordered north of the Chickahominy River to reinforce Porter. However, this measure proved to be too little, too late, as Lee's force was increasing in size and beginning to conduct more coordinated attacks. These assaults resulted in the rupture of Porter's defense and his corps' withdrawal south across the Chickahominy.[17]

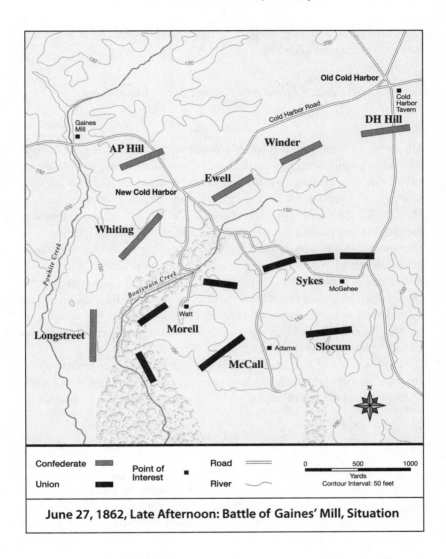

June 27, 1862, Late Afternoon: Battle of Gaines' Mill, Situation

On this afternoon McClellan gave up the opportunity to deploy a significant force north across the river to join Porter's corps on excellent defensive
terrain. Such a decision might have stalled or even defeated Lee's offensive
operation. In addition, the terrain was such that Federals could have conducted a successful defense and attacked Lee's exposed left (east) flank.

McClellan failed to use this opportunity to regain the tactical initiative.
He would never regain the initiative for the remainder of the Seven Days.
This critical decision initiated the operational pattern for his army for the

remainder of the Seven Days. His defensive-retreat frame of mind would lead him to the next critical decision.

McClellan Decides to Retreat to the James River

Situation

On June 26 Lee commenced his planned turning movement around McClellan's right (north) flank. Because Jackson's Command was not in position, this maneuver degenerated into a series of unsuccessful attacks against that part of Porter's Fifth Corps deployed along Beaver Dam Creek at Mechanicsville. Although Porter was successful, McClellan refused to reinforce him so that he could continue the defense, and maybe even counterattack, at that location. Ordered to withdraw, Porter moved his corps back to the high ground south of and overlooking Boatswain's Swamp (Creek). On June 27 Porter again, with minimal reinforcement, fought a defensive battle. Although McClellan had several opportunities to perhaps gain a Union victory by making this a stronger position or even counterattacking, he refused to do so. The day ended with Porter's troops driven off their defensive position and retreating south across the Chickahominy River.[18]

On the night of June 27, the Army of the Potomac's five infantry corps, the cavalry, and the reserve artillery were all located south of the Chickahominy River. McClellan needed to decide what his army would do next.

Options

McClellan had four options to choose from. He could retreat eastward toward White House Landing and West Point , move back down the Virginia Peninsula toward Fort Monroe, evacuate south across the Peninsula, or hold with his right and attack with his left to capture Richmond. If he retreated, McClellan would be moving not only the infantry, artillery, and cavalry combat elements of his army, but also an artillery siege train of 26 heavy guns, more than 3,800 wagons and ambulances, and a herd of 2,518 cattle.[19]

Option 1

McClellan could retreat to White House Landing and West Point. In doing so, he would be withdrawing along his railroad supply line to his forward supply base, and he would protect both of them. At White House Landing and West Point, the Pamunkey and York Rivers could continue to supply and reinforce the army. If necessary, the Federals could retreat farther to Fort Monroe on the tip of the Pninsula. From White House Landing and West

Point McClellan's troops could also retreat northeast for fourteen miles to Urbana, located near the mouth of the Rappahannock River. There, the army could continue to resupply for future land operations, or it could be removed by watercraft to another location. This option would partially accomplish what Lee intended with his turning movement. It would bring the Union army out from its siege position but not necessarily bring on a decisive battle.

Option 2

The Union commander could also retreat back to Fort Monroe on the tip of the Virginia Peninsula. This choice would have the army move back along the route of its previous advance toward Richmond. It could then be resupplied from the area of Fort Monroe. While retreating, Federal soldiers would pass through several locations where delaying actions might develop into defensive battles. Moreover, evacuating along this route would require crossing the Chickahominy River at some point, which might provide a choke point that would give Lee a tactical advantage. This option required the army to march the longest distance.

Option 3

McClellan could withdraw south across the Peninsula to the James River. Once there and in position, the Federals could use the river as a supply line. Gunboats on the James could also support the troops. While McClellan's army could retreat back to the tip of the Peninsula from this location, this area could also become a staging area for future offensive operation toward Richmond or Petersburg. There were a limited number of roads for the army to use to travel south. This circumstance might give Lee the opportunity to march elements of his army to cut the route of retreat.

Option 4

In addition, McClellan could hold with his right and attack to capture Richmond. After Porter's corps retreated south across the Chickahominy River, the Army of the Potomac was reunited, and the river provided a good defensive obstacle. Lee's army was divided into two parts: the force used for the attempted turning movement, which also fought the subsequent Battle of Gaines' Mill, and Magruder's holding force in front of Richmond. McClellan could establish a defensive line along the Chickahominy to hold that part of Lee's army north of the river. In the meantime, the remainder of his army could attack west against the smaller force in front of Richmond. McClellan would be using an interior line, while Lee would have exterior lines. The

Union commander would thus have the capability to shift troops faster. However, McClellan was in a defensive-retreat frame of mind, and it is doubtful that he ever seriously considered this option.

Decision

McClellan decided to retreat across the Virginia Peninsula to the James River. He tried to disguise this by calling the order a "change of base," but it was a retreat just the same. At the James River he would establish a position where his army could be supplied by water and supported by Union gunboats. From this location he might restart offensive operation against Richmond or Petersburg.

Results/Impact

The Federal retreat across the Virginia Peninsula was a gigantic undertaking. The roadnet was very limited, and most of the roads ran in the wrong direction. In addition, the Union army's combat strength, large wagon train, and herd of beeves had to cross a swamp and creek.[20]

During the night of June 27, McClellan issued orders for his army to retreat. Not all of his subordinate commanders believed this was the right decision. Brig. Gens. Philip Kearny and Joseph Hooker, division commanders

Brig. Gen. Phillip Kearny, USA.
Library of Congress.

Brig. Gen. Joseph Hooker, USA.
Library of Congress.

in the Third Corps, went to McClellan and told him that an attack against the thinly held Confederate lines in front of Richmond should be launched immediately. McClellan refused. In the ensuing argument, Kearny became so verbally aggressive toward McClellan that many present thought he would be arrested.[21]

The army started moving south toward the James River the next morning. This decision would set the tone and sequence of events for the remainder of the Seven Days. The immediate sequence of events following from this decision included a rearguard action at Savage Station, a Union defense at White Oak Swamp, a battle at the Glendale Crossroads, and a battle at Malvern Hill, then a retreat to Harrison's Landing on the James River.

With this decision McClellan gave up any real opportunity and thoughts of capturing Richmond or maneuvering to fight and seriously damage part of Lee's army. From this point on, the Union army faced a series of defensive actions, some of them successful, and retreat.

Alternate Decision/Scenario

After Gaines' Mill when Porter's Fifth Corps retreated across the Chickahominy River, the Army of the Potomac was all together south of the river. McClellan now had the opportunity to regain the tactical initiative and hit Lee a surprising and perhaps game changing blow. McClellan had five infantry corps. Porter could have been joined by one other corps and together a defensive position established just south of the Chickahominy, which would provide a natural obstacle to any attack. The other three corps could then be given the mission to attack the Confederate defenses in front of Richmond. Several senior Union commanders believed this attack would be successful. Lee's two separate parts of his army would be on exterior lines and require more time to shift forces. Adoption of this option would change the events following Gaines' Mill and created a definite shift in the historical time line.

CHAPTER 3

WHITE OAK SWAMP AND GLENDALE, JUNE 29–30, 1862

As the Army of the Potomac retreated south across the Virginia Peninsula, four critical decisions were made, all by Confederate commanders. One critical decision would move the Army of Northern Virginia from attempting a turning movement to conducting a pursuit, two negative critical decisions would prevent the Confederate army from applying its full combat power to the Union defenses at Glendale, and one critical decision would result in the rebels' misuse of a reserve.

Lee Decides on a Pursuit

Situation

On the night of June 27, Maj. Gen. Fitz John Porter's battered Fifth Corps retreated to the south side of the Chickahominy River, and then the bridges were destroyed. Lee's army remained divided into two segments: Magruder's four-division force holding the defenses of Richmond, and the six divisions north of the Chickahominy River that attempted the turning movement and now had lost contact with the Army of the Potomac.[1]

On June 28, leaving a strong rear guard at Savage Station, the Union army began a retreat across the Peninsula to the James River. The route of retreat

Chickahominy River at site of Grapevine Bridge. Author.

began at Savage Station, extended southeast and then south across White Oak Swamp, then went through the crossroads at Glendale, over Malvern Hill, and along the James River to Harrison's Landing. It was fourteen road miles to the James River, then seven more miles to Harrison's Landing for a total of twenty-one miles. As the road network facilitated movement along the Peninsula's length and not across it, the routes crossing to the James River were very limited and passed through choke points such as that at Glendale. McClellan would be moving not only a large infantry force with artillery, but also the artillery reserve, an artillery siege train of 26 heavy guns, more than 3,800 wagons and ambulances, and a herd of 2,518 cattle. An army of this size would make slow progress on the limited road system traversing the Peninsula.[2]

When Porter's troops crossed the Chickahominy River and the retreat commenced, Lee lost contact with the Army of the Potomac. He thought that McClellan might be heading for the James River, but he was not positive, as there were several other options. To ensure that McClellan had not ordered a retreat back down the Virginia Peninsula or to White House Landing, Lee sent Stuart's cavalry toward the Union supply base at White House. When Stuart reached Dispatch Station on the Richmond and York River Railroad, he found the bridge destroyed. Continuing on to White House, he found that large stocks of unevacuated supplies were burning. Ewell's Division had also been sent to Dispatch Station, and it was then ordered to Bottoms Bridge, which was the first place the Union army could cross the Chickahominy River if it was retreating down the Peninsula. Reconnaissance found no indication

Trent House, McClellan's headquarters June 12-28. Author.

of Union movement across this bridge, and Ewell's Division remained there to ensure that no Union forces attempted to cross. In addition, dust clouds and explosions of ammunition and supplies being destroyed pointed to a Federal retreat across the Peninsula. Such intelligence led Lee to deduce that McClellan was retreating to the James River.[3]

Maj. Gen. Richard S. Ewell, CSA.
Library of Congress.

Options

When indicators showed that the Army of the Potomac was retreating across the Peninsula to the James River, Lee had three options: conduct a pursuit, follow and maintain direct pressure, or hold in place.

Option 1

Lee could send his forces on a pursuit, one of the four types of offensive operations.[4] A pursuit focuses on the enemy force and has two components: a force that keeps pressure on the rear of the retreating enemy, and a force that maneuvers to cut the route of retreat, thus trapping all or part of the opposition's soldiers. To conduct a pursuit Lee would have part of his army apply direct pressure on the rear of the retreating Union column. This would cause the rear guard and perhaps reinforcements to protect the retreating column by stopping and fighting before moving on. As a result, the maneuver force would have time to cut the route of retreat and trap all or a significant part of McClellan's army. The Confederate units would be marching on separate roads, and, importantly, none of them would have to cross the route of any others. Selecting this option could possibly accomplish Lee's operational goal, but it would require close and continuous coordination and communication between the force applying direct pressure and the force engaged in maneuvering.

Option 2

Lee could also follow and directly pressure McClellan's troops. If he decided on this option, Lee would aggressively trail and attack the Union army's rear guard and supports whenever possible. If this action was successful, units from the retreating column might turn back to reinforce the rear guard, possibly resulting in another battle and the opportunity for Lee to further damage the Army of the Potomac. This option would allow Lee to keep his army together, and if McClellan occupied a defensive position, the Confederate army could concentrate against it. This course of action would not allow Lee to cut off McClellan's retreat, but he might inflict extensive damage to the Union army as it retreated to the James River.

Option 3

Finally, Lee's army could hold in place, remaining in the positions they occupied on June 28 and allowing the Army of the Potomac to continue unmolested to a position on the James River. Stuart's cavalry could follow, report on McClellan's progress, and alert Lee to any Union change in direction. By holding in place Lee would be able to rest and resupply his troops and still be in a position between Richmond and McClellan's force. Except for Stuart's cavalry, Lee would break contact with the Union forces and surrender any opportunity to continue to attack them and do further damage. While the Union army would be driven away from Richmond, it would still be a viable force and located to recommence operation toward the capital from a different direction.

Decision

Lee decided on the most aggressive of these options—conducting a pursuit. This choice gave him the best opportunity to cut off all or part of McClellan's army. If the pursuit was successful, it would compel the Union army to either attack or defend, and it would provide Lee the opportunity to destroy the enemy force or cause enough harm to render all or part of it combat ineffective.

Results/Impact

Lee planned for the Army of Northern Virginia to effect a general concentration southward from the edge of White Oak Swamp to the James River and parallel to the north–south roads McClellan was using. The simultaneous convergence of four columns would be difficult, but it was possible.[5]

In conducting the pursuit, Maj. Gen. John B. Magruder's command (three divisions) was to move east, parallel to the Williamsburg Road and the Richmond and York River Railroad, and attack the rear of the Union army, which was in the vicinity of Savage Station. After rebuilding Grapevine Bridge, Maj. Gen. Thomas J. "Stonewall" Jackson's command (two divisions)[6] plus Maj. Gen. Daniel H. Hill's division was to cross the Chickahominy River and support Magruder. Magruder and Jackson, as the direct pressure force, were to hold as much of the Army of the Potomac as they could in place.[7]

The maneuver force consisted of Huger's, A. P. Hill's, Longstreet's, and Holmes's Divisions. Maj. Gen. Benjamin Huger's men were to march down the Charles City Road toward the crossroads at Glendale. Maj. Gens. Ambrose P. Hill's and James Longstreet's units had the longest distance to march. They were to cross the Chickahominy River at New Bridge, pass behind Magruder's Command, and march south to the Darbytown Road. Once on the Darbytown Road, these divisions were to march southeast to the intersection with the Long Bridge Road, turn left, and march northeast toward Glendale. The Glendale Crossroads was a choke point that the retreating Union army had to pass through. Hill and Longstreet were to come up on Huger's right, and all three divisions would attack the head of the retreating

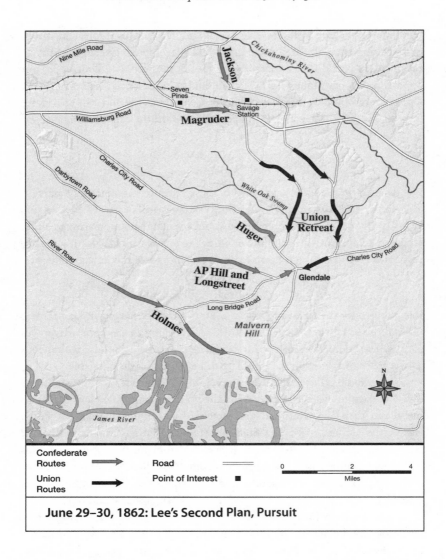

June 29–30, 1862: Lee's Second Plan, Pursuit

Union column or break it if the lead units had already passed. To further cut the route of retreat, Maj. Gen. Theophilus Holmes was to march his division along the River Road to New Market and then to Malvern Hill.[8]

If each Confederate column was successful, Lee's army would close on and engage McClellan's in the following order: extreme right, Holmes; right and center, Longstreet and A. P. Hill; left, Huger; rear of the enemy, Jackson and Magruder. Magruder's Division was later rerouted so as to support Longstreet and A. P. Hill. More on this later.[9]

The Army of the Potomac was on the march. Keyes's Fourth Corps was leading, followed by Brig. Gen. Fitz John Porter's Fifth Corps, the artillery reserve, the supply train, and later Brig. Gen. Samuel P. Heintzelman's Third Corps. Elements of Brig. Gen. Edwin V. Sumner's Second Corps and Brig. Gen. William B. Franklin's Sixth Corps formed the rear guard at Savage Station, which Magruder made contact with and attacked. Jackson's command did not make it across the river. With insufficient combat power, Magruder was stopped by the rear guard, which then left to follow the rest of the army. The direct pressure force was unable to stop the Union retreat or hold the rear guard in place, but the maneuver force was marching toward the Glendale choke point.[10]

Lee decision to conduct a pursuit ensured that his offensive operations would continue. His choice would establish the sequence of events for the next day and create situations that would cause two more critical decisions. Had Lee chosen differently, the June 30 and July 1 events probably would not have occurred. Operations would possibly have stagnated or come to a halt, and the Seven Days would not have continued.

Jackson Decides Not to Cross White Oak Swamp

Situation

After crossing the Chickahominy River, the next terrain obstacle for Jackson was White Oak Swamp. The marshy watercourse ran generally southeast, and any force moving south from Savage Station to the James River had to cross it. Crossing could only be accomplished at White Oak Bridge and at several fords west of the bridge. Both the high ground to the south and the swamp provided a natural and strong defensive position. The bridge crossing was only 2.3 road miles from the critical Glendale intersection of the Long Bridge Road, Willis Church Road, and Charles City Road. The entire Union army had to pass through this intersection and then south to Malvern Hill.[11]

Jackson's task in Lee's plan was to maintain contact with and apply pressure on the Union rear guard. In addition, if the situation presented itself, Jackson and his men were to attack and destroy or damage the rear guard. Early in the morning of June 30, Jackson's Command[12] with D. H. Hill's Division leading finally crossed the Chickahominy River and proceeded through Savage Station, then along the White Oak Road to White Oak Bridge. Previously, the Army of the Potomac's rear guard had marched south on this same road. After crossing White Oak Swamp, the Federals destroyed the bridge and occupied positions on the higher ground overlooking the crossing from the south. The rear guard at this location was commanded by Brig. Gen. William B. Franklin, the Sixth Corps commander, and it consisted of Brig. Gen. William F. Smith's Second Division of the Sixth Corps, Brig. Gen. Israel B. Richardson's First Division of the Second Corps, and Brig. Gen. Henry M. Naglee's First Brigade from the Fourth Corps' Second Division.[13]

Just before noon elements from D. H. Hill's Division began arriving north of White Oak Swamp, where they discovered the bridge had been destroyed and Union troops were in position south of the swamp. Col. Stapleton Crutchfield, Jackson's chief of artillery, arrived and began deploying artillery to the right (west) of the road. He positioned thirty-one guns and opened fire on the Union positions at 1:45 p.m.[14]

Under the covering fire of the artillery, Jackson and D. H. Hill conducted a reconnaissance but were forced back by Union rifle fire. Col. Thomas Munford and his Second Virginia Cavalry then received orders to carry out reconnaissance along the watercourse. Munford moved to the east (left) and after about a half mile found a little-used crossing that was undefended. He reported this to Jackson. In the meantime, Brig. Gen. Wade Hampton had brought his brigade forward and then on his own had made a reconnaissance to the east. At a shorter distance than the crossing Munford found, Hampton discovered a shallow area that could be hastily bridged and crossed by infantry. Crossing at this point would place Hampton's troops on the right (east) flank of W. F. Smith's position. This information was reported to Jackson, who told Hampton

Col. Thomas Munford, CSA.
Library of Congress.

Brig. Gen. Wade Hampton, CSA.
National Archives.

to build the bridge. Although three fords (Brackett's, Fisher's, and Jordan's) were located within three and one-half miles west of the destroyed bridge, no reconnaissance was ordered in that direction.[15]

Jackson now faced with a situation requiring a Decision.

Options

Confronting a Union force and the destroyed White Oak Bridge, Jackson had two options: attack or hold in position and engage with artillery.

Option 1

In keeping with Lee's operational intent for him to maintain pressure on the Union rear guard, Jackson could attack. Crossing White Oak Swamp via the crossing to the east would place Confederate forces in position to hit the Union defenders' flank. Such an attack would cause continued damage to these units. It might also unhinge the Federals' position and force the rear guard back toward the fighting then in progress around the Glendale Crossroads. This, in turn, would place those defenders under attack or threat of attack from two separate directions.

Option 2

Alternatively, Jackson could hold his infantry in their current position but continue to engage the Union forces with artillery. Although not a very

Maj. Gen. Thomas J. "Stonewall" Jackson, CSA. Library of Congress.

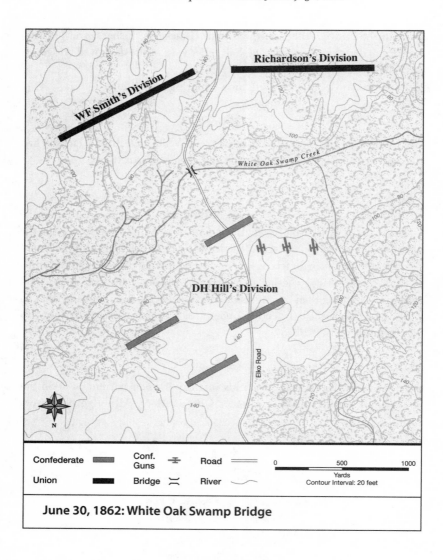

June 30, 1862: White Oak Swamp Bridge

aggressive option, this course of action might keep the Union defenders in place. However, if the threat was not substantial, part of the enemy force might be sent to reinforce the units fighting at the Glendale Crossroads.

Decision

Jackson by default chose Option 2. When he didn't issue any orders to his waiting infantry and artillery, he essentially decided to do nothing.

Results/Impact

Just over two miles from Jackson's position, A. P. Hill's and Longstreet's Divisions were engaged in desperate attacks against Union defenders holding open their route of retreat to the James River. Jackson's failure to move against the enemy soldiers at White Oak Bridge prevented a Confederate threat from developing in the rear of the Glendale position. In addition, two brigades of Brig. Gen. John Sedgwick's Second Division, Second Corps that had been sent to reinforce the Union troops at White Oak Bridge were recalled back to the Willis Church Road. They arrived there in time to counterattack and stop a developing Confederate breakthrough.[16]

Jackson's inaction kept three divisions (D. H. Hill's, Whiting's, and Winder's) out of the Glendale Crossroads battle, where they might have been enough for a Confederate victory. It nullified a major segment of Lee's plan and contributed to the Union army's survival at Glendale Crossroads, followed by a repositioning to Malvern Hill. In conjunction with the next critical decision, this choice would ultimately prove a major part in the failure of Lee's pursuit.

Huger Decides Not to Attack

Situation

On June 30 Lee's second plan, a pursuit to cut off all or part of the Union army and destroy it, was reaching the point of another battle.

McClellan's army was centered on the Glendale Crossroads, where four corps with a total of nine infantry divisions were deployed. The left of the position was anchored on Malvern Hill. From that location a mile-long gap stretched north along the Willis Church Road. Just prior to Willis Methodist Church, the line of troops began again and extended one mile to the Glendale Crossroads, then beyond for about a third of a mile. From the Glendale Crossroads the position then went in a northeasterly direction for two miles to White Oak Swamp Bridge. This was the right of the defenses. The line generally formed an upside-down L, which gave the Union force interior lines on the defensive position.[17]

Benjamin Huger graduated from the US Military Academy in 1825 at the age of twenty. He spent the next thirty-six years in various assignments, including command of arsenals and chief of ordnance for Gen. Winfield Scott in Mexico. Upon the fall of Fort Sumter, Huger resigned his commission, entered Confederate service as a brigadier general on June 17, 1861, and was promoted to major general on October 7, 1861. He commanded the department

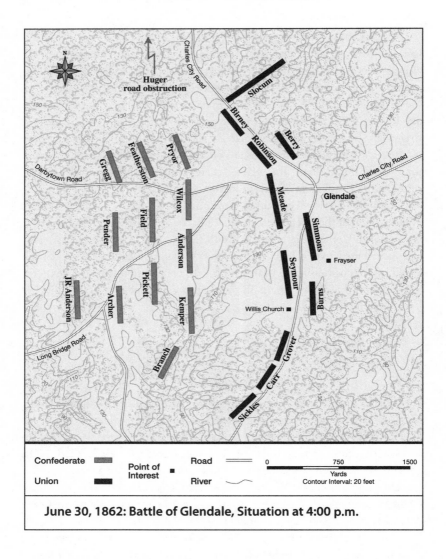

June 30, 1862: Battle of Glendale, Situation at 4:00 p.m.

that included Norfolk Navy Yard, which he destroyed along with the ironclad *Merrimac (Virginia)* when ordered to evacuate. His force repositioned to the vicinity of Richmond, where he commanded it during Seven Pines and the Seven Days. In July 1862 Huger was relieved of his command and assigned as an inspector of artillery and ordnance in the Trans-Mississippi Department. After the war he lived in Fauquier County, Virginia. Huger died in 1877.[18]

Early in the morning Lee had four separate columns converging on the Army of the Potomac's four corps. Jackson's Command, with two of his three

Maj. Gen. Benjamin Huger, CSA.
Library of Congress.

divisions and reinforcement from D. H. Hill's Division, was supposed to bring direct pressure on the Union rear guard now at White Oak Swamp Bridge. To Jackson's right Maj. Gen. Benjamin Huger's division was advancing on the Charles City Road to attack the Union defenders at the Glendale Crossroads.

Farther to the right, Longstreet's and A. P. Hill's Divisions were marching to strike the Union position from the west. Even farther right, Maj. Gen. Theophilus H. Holmes's division was moving parallel to the James River along the River Road with the intent of interfering with McClellan's trains as they crossed Malvern Hill. Magruder's Division had turned back from Savage Station and was following Longstreet and A. P. Hill with orders to be prepared to support them.[19]

Led by D. H. Hill's Division, Jackson's Command advanced to the White Oak Swamp Bridge, where, as previously discussed, it was idle for the rest of the day.

Huger's Division spent the night along the Charles City Road about three miles from the Glendale Crossroads. The next morning (June 30) the division, with Brig. Gen. William Mahone's brigade leading, resumed the march toward Glendale on the Charles City Road. After a mile they came upon felled trees that obstructed the road. Huger had to continue moving south toward Glendale and attack the Union position with Longstreet and A. P. Hill.[20]

Options

Confronted by the blocked road, Huger had two options: clear the obstacles from his path or cut a parallel route through the woods.

Option 1

Huger could order troops, under cover of skirmishers, to clear the road of the felled trees. Someone inspecting the site later stated that a company could have done this in a reasonable amount of time. The trees were an obstacle only for the artillery and supply wagons; with some difficulty, the infantry could continue down the road about a mile until the obstacle ended. The artillery and wagons could then follow on as the road was opened. This course of action had the advantage of keeping Huger's Division moving toward the Glendale Crossroads and placing it in position to attack with Longstreet and A. P. Hill.

Option 2

Brig. Gen. William Mahone had suggested cutting a parallel road through the woods. As with the Charles City Road, this newly created route was not necessary for the infantry to continue moving forward. It was primarily for the artillery and supply wagons. Constructing a new road would be a time-consuming task. As fast as Confederates cut the new path, Union troops could continue to fell trees into the Charles City Road and increase the distance the new road would have to extend. This circumstance could result in a never-ending cycle that would remain unresolved until the lead Confederate units came to open fields, where an obstructed road would not matter. Choosing this option would effectively remove Huger's Division from Lee's plan.

Decision

Huger decided to accept Mahone's recommendation and cut a parallel road through the woods.

Results/Impact

Huger's decision committed his division to a snail's-pace advance toward the Glendale Crossroads. As Huger's men cleared the new route, Union troops continued to cut trees and extend the Charles City Road obstacle. This required the Confederates to cut an even longer road than they had initially needed. The rebels had insufficient tools for the job, so it took most of the day for the road to reach a location where the forest ended. When Huger's troops were past the obstacle and back on the Charles City Road, it was almost night, too late to join the Glendale battle, and the march was halted.[21]

Charles City Road through a heavy wood, similar to 1862. Author.

This decision prevented Huger's Division from contributing to Lee's plan to cut off the retreat of all or part of the Army of the Potomac by attacking the Union defenses at Glendale and along the Willis Church Road with Longstreet and A. P. Hill.

In conjunction with Jackson's inactivity at White Oak Swamp Bridge, Huger's failure to reach his assigned position and attack removed four key divisions from actively participating in Lee's plan and reduced the attacking force by one-half. This was a significant enough reduction in combat power to give the defenders the edge they needed to be successful. In addition, unengaged Union units were redeployed and committed to sections of the defensive position where potential breakthroughs developed.

Magruder Is Ordered to Support Holmes

Situation

As part of his pursuit plan, Lee had ordered Maj. Gen. Theophilus H. Holmes to march his division on the River Road, parallel to the James River, toward Malvern Hill. While he was with Longstreet, Lee received a report of Union troops on Malvern Hill and wagons crossing over the hill and on toward the James River.[22]

Lee decided to investigate and rode south to Holmes's location, where he verified the earlier report. Concerned that McClellan might be slipping

Maj. Gen. Theophilus H. Holmes, CSA.
National Archives.

through the trap, he ordered Holmes to bring up artillery (six rifle guns) and deploy infantry against the position.[23]

What Lee probably did not realize was that Malvern Hill was developing into a strong Union defensive position, especially on the western side, where a fifty-foot vertical bluff rose from the lower ground Holmes's Division occupied. Sykes's three-brigade division with two batteries of artillery was deployed at the top of this bluff. Sykes could be reinforced by all or part of Morell's division with three infantry brigades and four batteries. In addition, the Army Artillery Reserve with ten of its sixteen batteries was available for additional support.[24] All in all, this was a very formidable position that Holmes's Division could not be expected to successfully attack.[25]

The day before, Maj. Gen. John B. Magruder's division had been part of the force keeping pressure on the Union rear guard and had participated in the fight at Savage Station. On June 30 Lee had ordered Magruder to turn back from Savage Station, follow Longstreet and A. P. Hill, and be prepared to support them. While Lee was observing the Malvern Hill position, Magruder's men were marching southeast on the Darbytown Road.[26]

Magruder's Division was the only army-level reserve immediately available; Lee now had to decide where to commit it. Such a decision would probably determine the outcome of the fighting on June 30.

Options

A commander influences a combat operation in four ways: weighting the main attack, establishing priority of supporting fires, ensuring timely commitment of the reserve, and maintaining a personal presence. Lee was now in the position of deciding how the reserve, Magruder's Division, would be committed.[27] This determination would have a major impact on the fighting on June 30.

Lee could either order the reserve to support Longstreet's and A. P. Hill's attack against the Union position along the Willis Church Road, or commit the force to support Holmes's attack against the west side of Malvern Hill.

Option 1

The Confederate reserve could reinforce Longstreet and A. P. Hill, who were to launch the main assault on the Union position at the Glendale Crossroads and along the Willis Church Road.[28] Huger's Division was also to be part of this attack, but his troops did not get there in time to participate. The two divisions that did strike only had a marginal superiority at the point of contact. Therefore, it might be necessary to commit the rebel reserve to support and capitalize on any offensive success. A clear victory in this area would cut the Union army's route of retreat and isolate those units north of the break. This option supported Lee's overall objective in fighting on June 30.

Option 2

Alternatively, Lee could send the reserve to support Holmes's attack. At best, Holmes's offensive against the Malvern Hill western position was a supporting attack.[29] To have even a minimal chance of success, his troops would require assistance from the rebel army reserve. Sending additional forces to support Holmes would violate the principle of retaining the reserve's commitment for the main attack or in case of an unforeseeable major success by a supporting attack. Even if Holmes's assault was successful, it would not necessarily ensure the accomplishment of Lee's main objective.

Decision

Lee decided on Option 2 and ordered Magruder to change his direction of march and move south to support Holmes.

Results/Impact

Lee's decisions immediately impacted the combat on June 30. Holmes had deployed six rifled guns against the Union's western position on Malvern

Hill, and he also brought up some of his infantry as supports. His guns opened fire between 4:00 and 5:00 p.m. The overwhelming Union artillery response, including two gunboats on the James River, dispersed Holmes's artillery and panicked his infantry, much of which fled back to the west. About the time this was happening, Longstreet and then A. P. Hill began their attack against the Union position at Glendale Crossroads and along the Willis Church Road.[30]

Magruder received an order at 2:00 p.m. while his division was marching along the Darbytown Road; he was to halt and rest his men but be prepared to move at any time. Magruder's Division was now about four miles from the soon-to-commence combat for the Glendale Crossroads, and he occupied a good reserve position from which to be committed to reinforce that fight. While at this location Magruder received the order to move farther south and support Holmes. In the meantime, Longstreet commenced his attack at Glendale–Willis Church Road.[31]

About 6:30 p.m., while his division was marching south, Magruder was commanded to send half of his troops to the Glendale fight, which he did. This was followed by another order to bring all of his soldiers to the Glendale fight, and he complied with this order as well, but it was too late. When the division arrived, Magruder received word that his men were to relieve Longstreet's troops. His force completed this task at 3:00 a.m.[32]

Maj. Gen. James Longstreet, CSA.
National Archives.

During Longstreet's and A. P. Hill's attacks, the Union defense found itself almost penetrated or close to collapse in several locations. However, neither Longstreet nor Hill had sufficient force to take advantage of this situation. Had a reserve been available, its commitment might have changed the course of events, severed the Union route of retreat, and cut off a significant amount of the Army of the Potomac with disastrous results.[33]

Lee's decision removed another division from his attack and together with Jackson's and Huger's four divisions resulted in a major portion of Lee's army (five divisions with seventeen infantry brigades and twenty-three artillery batteries) not getting into action. It allowed a successful Union defense followed by a march to Malvern Hill.

The inability of Lee and his subordinates to accomplish the plan for June 30 would push the fighting into one more day.

CHAPTER 4

MALVERN HILL AND RETREAT, JULY 1, 1862, AND BEYOND

Three critical decisions were made during the time period this chapter covers. One of them would result in one of the bloodiest battles of the Seven Days, and another one would ignore a tactical advantage gained by a victory. Still another decision would bring a final end to the Peninsula Campaign and the Seven Days and have a far-reaching impact for the remainder of 1862 and beyond.

Lee Orders an Attack

Situation

The Union defensive position on Malvern Hill began forming on June 30 with the arrival of two divisions of the Fifth Corps and the majority of the army's artillery reserve. At the end of the fighting at White Oak Swamp Bridge, Glendale, and the Willis Church Road, the Union defenders continued marching south. As they approached the hill, the Second and Third Corps went into defensive positions. The Sixth Corps marched south over the hill and joined Peck's division at locations on and near the River Road.[1]

When the defenses were finalized the Fifth Corps had two divisions in place. Sykes's division faced west. The most likely Confederate avenue of approach was from the north and was covered by Brig. Gen. George W. Morell's division and Brig. Gen. Darius N. Couch's Fourth Corps' division. Morell's division was positioned from Sykes's right to the Willis Church Road. Couch's division was to the right of Morell's. Sumner's Second Corps and Heintzelman's Third Corps were located behind Couch and facing east, but they could easily send units to reinforce Morell and Couch. Col. Henry J. Hunt's artillery reserve was positioned in an assembly area a short distance behind the infantry. From there, batteries could reinforce the defensive line, and ammunition could be resupplied.[2]

During the morning and early afternoon, Confederate units marched south from the previous day's fight and moved into positions from which to attack. D. H. Hill's Division traveled the Willis Church Road to a location astride the road and nine hundred yards from the center and right of the Union defenses. Winder's and Whiting's Divisions followed and deployed behind D. H. Hill.[3]

The Carter's Mill Road running from northwest to southeast intersected the Willis Church Road five hundred yards in front of the Union center. Brig. Gens. Lewis A. Armistead's and Ambrose Wright's brigades of Huger's Division marched on this road and deployed to its right one thousand yards from the left half of the Union defenses.[4]

After proceeding along the wrong road, Magruder's Division retraced its steps, then marched on the Carter's Mill Road, arrived shortly after 3:00

Brig. Gen. Lewis A. Armistead, CSA.
National Archives.

Brig. Gen. Ambrose R. Wright, CSA.
Library of Congress.

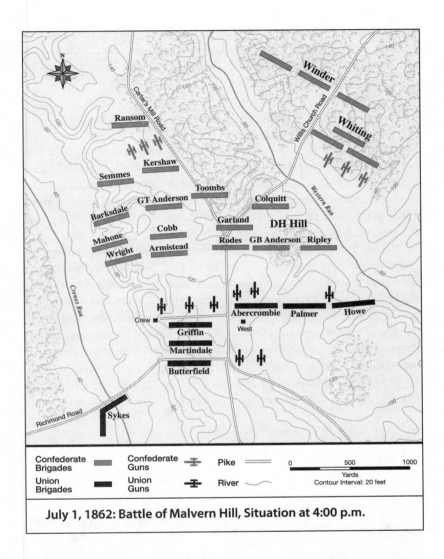

July 1, 1862: Battle of Malvern Hill, Situation at 4:00 p.m.

p.m., and took position behind Armistead and Wright. Following Huger, Brig. Gen. David R. Jones and Maj. Gen. Lafayette McLaws arrived and deployed behind Huger's Division.[5]

When D. H. Hill, William Whiting, Charles Winder, Benjamin Huger, John Magruder, David R. Jones, and Lafayette McLaws finished deploying, Lee had twenty-one brigades in place to attack.[6]

Sometime between noon and early afternoon Col. Robert H. Chilton of Lee's staff wrote and issued this order:

Batteries have been established to rake the enemy's lines. If it is broken, as is probable, Armstead, who can witness the effect of the fire, has been ordered to charge with a yell. Do the same.

R. H. Chilton
Assistant Adjutant-General.[7]

Poorly conceived and written, this order is a classic example of what not to do. No time shows when it was composed. The choice of a yell, even by a brigade, to indicate that all units should attack is problematic, and designating a brigade commander to determine whether the major portion of an army should attack is a nonstarter. Later in the day, this directive caused more confusion than it provided command and control.

Earlier, Lee and Longstreet had attempted to establish two artillery concentrations of fifty guns each on the left and right of the Confederate position. They believed these guns would provide such a volume of cross fire on the Federals that they would withdraw their defending artillery. On the right only four batteries (twenty guns) went into the firing position, while on the left five of ten batteries were in place. None of these batteries went into position or fired weapons at the same time, and Union artillery fire successively overwhelmed them as a result.[8]

When the massed artillery cross fire from the Confederate left and right failed to develop, Lee again rode to the left (east) side of his position to look

Malvern Hill as seen from the Confederate left. Author.

Brig. Gen. William H. C. Whiting,
CSA. National Archives.

for a way to attack the Union right flank. While at that location, which did
not provide him a view of the battlefield, Lee was informed that Magruder's
Division had arrived and deployed. He also received an incorrect report that
Armistead was apparently moving forward. At about the same time, Whiting,
who had observed some Union batteries departing the firing line to resupply ammunition, and who thought the Confederate artillery had successfully
driven back the Union guns, sent Lee a message erroneously reporting as
much. The Confederate commander probably received all of this information
at about 4:00 p.m. or later.[9]

Malvern Hill as seen from the Confederate right. Author.

Lee knew that July 1 was probably the last day in which he could severely damage or even defeat the Army of the Potomac. Once the Union army left Malvern Hill it would concentrate in its entirety at some point on the James River, probably with secure flanks on the river. There, it could be resupplied, reinforced, and supported by Federal gunboats. Thinking that he still might be able to attack, even in the late afternoon, Lee had a decision to make.

Options

Presented with an unexpected possible development, Lee could either order an immediate attack or ride to a location where he could view the battlefield and verify Whiting's and Magruder's reports.

Option 1

Lee could order his troops to attack at once. Sunset on July 1 was at 6:07 p.m., and it would be dark by 6:30 p.m. It would require a short period of time to get the attack order to Magruder and have the other commanders to follow his lead. Ordering an immediate assault would ensure that it would be launched and have sufficient daylight to be carried out. However, Lee would be relying solely on Whiting's and Magruder's interpretations of events. If those two men were incorrect, then the Confederate infantry could be conducting a frontal assault against a very strong Union defense.[10]

Option 2

On the other hand, Lee could verify Whiting's and Magruder's reports before ordering an attack. This option would require some additional time for Lee to ride to a location (fifteen to thirty minutes) and then observe the battlefield to determine the situation. However, the Confederate commander could use his own observations to decide whether to launch an assault. Although this course of action would use up some of the limited daylight, Lee would be sure the Union artillery was withdrawing, which was a prelude to the infantry withdrawing, and the attack would thus have some chance of success and not be a frontal assault against a strong defense. If Lee chose to attack, some time was still left for his troops to do so. If the attack was successful, there probably would not be sufficient daylight for the rebels to pursue the retreating Federals.

Decision

Without seeing the current situation on the battlefield, Lee opted to order an immediate attack. To initiate this assault, he ordered Magruder "to advance rapidly," stating, "The enemy is getting off. Press forward your whole line and follow up on Armistead's success." This decision had drastic consequences beyond anything Lee could have imagined.[11]

Results/Impact

When Magruder directed the first line of troops on the right to attack, he instigated the battle for Malvern Hill. The first strike by the Confederate right involved four brigades (Armistead's, Wright's, Mahone's, and Cobb's). On the Confederate left, D. H. Hill attacked shortly thereafter with four of his brigades (Garland's, Gordon's, G. B. Anderson's, and Ripley's), while Colquitt's Brigade followed in support.[12]

On the right, Federals repulsed the first attacks, and the rebels committed two more brigades to the fight (Barksdale's and G. T. Anderson's). These forces were unable to push the attack to a successful conclusion. Three other brigades soon reinforced them (Ransom's, Semmes's, and Kershaw's), but they, too, were unsuccessful. In the evening twilight the attacks ceased.[13]

Meanwhile on the left, D. H. Hill's attack was repulsed. Jackson's (Winder's) and Ewell's Divisions were ordered forward, but the clogged road and the approaching night prevented any of those troops from reinforcing D. H. Hill.[14]

Maj. Gen. Daniel H. Hill, CSA.
Library of Congress.

Of the twenty-one brigades in position to participate in the attack, fourteen made it into the fight. These brigades accounted for 66 percent of the available force. Seven brigades did not make an assault; they were 34 percent of the available force, and six of these units were on the left behind D. H. Hill. Their absence greatly reduced the power of the attack on the left.[15]

With Lee's late-afternoon decision to attack and his subsequent defeat, his troops lost their last chance to inflict unsustainable damage on McClellan's army or prevent it from reaching a safe enclave on the James River. Although neither commander realized it at the time, this engagement was the last of the Seven Days Battles.

McClellan Retreats Again

Situation

As darkness descended on the battlefield, it was obvious to all that the Army of the Potomac had gained a decisive victory over the Army of Northern Virginia. The fight for Malvern Hill ended in a resounding Confederate defeat. Lee's army had taken part in its second-bloodiest fight of the Seven Days, incurring 5,650 casualties. Gaines' Mill was the army's bloodiest fight; it resulted in 7,993 casualties. Lee's losses at Malvern Hill were 28 percent of his total losses for the Seven Days' Battles. Combined with the 3,673 casualties from the White Oak Swamp Bridge–Glendale–Willis Church Road fight the day before, the Malvern Hill casualties brought Lee's losses in two days to 9,323. This figure was equal to 46 percent of total casualties.[16] Union losses amounted to 3,797 on June 30 and 3,007 on July 1, or about 72 percent of what Lee's were. Lee's army began the Seven Days with about 92,000 troops. With total casualties being 20,204 at the end of July 1, he had thus lost 22 percent of his troops' strength.[17]

Union troops still occupied their strong defensive positions on the hill. Two divisions of the Fifth Corps and Couch's division of the Fourth Corps continued to defend to the west and north. The Second and Third Corps remained in position facing to the east. During the fighting the Second Corps had two of six brigades engaged, while the Third Corps had one of six brigades engaged. The other division (two brigades) of the Fourth Corps was positioned south of Malvern Hill, and with the two divisions (six brigades) of the Sixth Corps it was securing the River Road area. The batteries of the artillery reserve were either deployed or in their assembly area behind the infantry.[18]

After a clear victory at Malvern Hill, McClellan had to decide what to do next.

Options

McClellan had three options to consider: remain in position, counterattack, or continue to retreat.

Option 1

McClellan might hold his troops in place. The Army of the Potomac had won a clear victory over its opponent, inflicting 5,650 casualties and suffering 3,007 of its own. Combined with casualties from the day before, these losses did not forebode well for Lee. If the casualty rate continued at this ratio, his army would be combat ineffective long before McClellan's. The Federals still occupied a strong defensive position, with protected flanks, that no Confederate unit had been able to penetrate. Of the Army of the Potomac's thirty-two infantry brigades, only eight had been heavily involved in the fighting. Substantial reserves were available to reinforce the Union troops where and when they were needed. By remaining in position, McClellan would continue to dominate the battlefield, maybe provoking Lee to attack again, or maybe gaining time to determine if a counterattack was feasible.

Option 2

His army having fought a successful defense, McClellan could also decide to counterattack. This option involved several courses of action. The Union commander could conduct a frontal assault against Lee's position, although this could prove to be the costliest choice. He could use the defenses to demonstrate and hold the Confederates in place while a large force carried out an envelopment. An envelopment of Lee's right (west) flank would offer the best chance of Union success. Federal forces could mass on the back side of Malvern Hill, where they could not be observed. They could then use the River Road to move to a location from which they could maneuver north until they could strike the Confederate right flank. Their attack would signal the forces in the defensive position to advance and maintain pressure on Lee's troops. Likewise, Union soldiers might conduct a similar envelopment against Lee's left (east) flank. In this case, however, the attack would have to cross Western Run and perhaps Turkey Run and the adjacent swampy areas.

Option 3

McClellan's final option was continuing to retreat to Harrison's Landing on the James River. While this would be the least risky decision, it would force Federals to give up all the tactical advantage they had gained from the

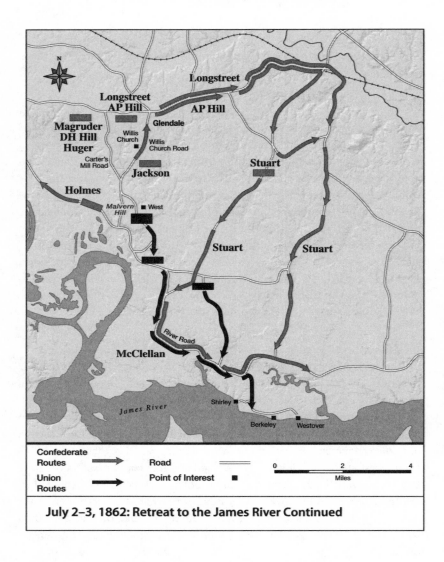

July 2–3, 1862: Retreat to the James River Continued

defensive fights on June 30 and July 1. This choice would return the tactical initiative to Lee.

Decision

Continuing the course of action he had adopted on June 27, McClellan ordered his army to retreat. Many officers and men thought this was a mistake and verbally voiced their displeasure with the commanding general. Even

McClellan's friend Fitz John Porter strongly favored a counterattack, and the fiery Philip Kearny told the other Third Corps' generals, "Such an order [to retreat] can only be prompted by cowardice or treason."[19]

Results/Impact

The Federals began their seven-mile retreat during the night of July 1 and carried on throughout the next day. The retreat demoralized the army, and a pouring rain exacerbated this effect. Troops engaged in a lot of straggling, marking the route of retreat with their discarded weapons, equipment, and wagons.[20]

Upon arriving at Harrison's Landing, the army occupied a four-mile-wide and one-mile-deep position backed up to the James River. The flanks were anchored on two creeks and swampland. Ninety thousand troops, 288 guns, 3,000 wagons and ambulances, 2,500 beef cattle, and 27,000 horses and mules were packed into this space. This crowding would soon cause sanitation and medical problems.[21]

Late on July 3 following Confederate units began to close on the Union position. The next day, Lee made a reconnaissance and decided not to attack. Leaving a force to observe the Union army, the rebel commander then moved his army back toward Richmond.[22]

McClellan's decision gave up any tactical advantages he had gained on July 1 and essentially brought the Seven Days' Battles to a close.

Alternate Decision/Scenario

Having won a significant defensive victory, McClellan had the opportunity of inflict additional casualties on Lee's army by remaining in position on Malvern Hill. This decision provided several courses of action: remain on the defense or counterattack (Options 1 and 2). If Federal army remained in position at least one more day Lee might bring up units that had not been engaged, additional artillery, and conduct another attack. However, having failed in one frontal attack he might attempt to maneuver around one of McClellan's flanks. Conversely McClellan would also have to opportunity to counterattack. The best choice would have been to maneuver and attack Lee's right (west) flank while the troops on Malvern Hill demonstrated to hold the Confederates in position. In any event, the Seven Days would have been extended for one or more days and might have had a different ending.

Halleck Decides to Evacuate the Peninsula

Situation

Early in July Abraham Lincoln visited McClellan at Harrison's Landing. The president wanted to see the Army of the Potomac and to discuss McClellan's next move. Nothing definitive came from this visit. Upon returning to Washington, Lincoln ordered Maj. Gen. Henry W. Halleck to the nation's capital and appointed him general-in-chief.[23]

Halleck was born in Westernville, New York, in 1815. He graduated third in his US Military Academy class in 1839 and toured French fortifications in 1844. Halleck later presented a series of lectures subsequently published as *Elements of Military Art and Science* and widely read by army officers. During and after the Mexican War he served in California, and in 1854 he resigned his commission to practice law. With the commencement of the Civil War, Halleck was appointed a major general in the regular army. His initial service was in the Western Theater. In July 1862 Lincoln brought Halleck to Washington and appointed him general-in-chief, a position he held until Ulysses S. Grant replaced him in March 1864. Halleck served the rest of the war as Grant's chief of staff, and after the fighting ended, he commanded the Department of the Pacific and then the Department of the South. While serving in this position he died in 1872.[24]

Berkley Plantation House at Harrison's Landing. Author.

Maj. Gen. Henry W. Halleck, USA.
Library of Congress.

During the summer of 1862 a second Union army was formed in north-ern Virginia. That spring four significant Union field forces were stationed in the state, and the largest was the Army of the Potomac. Maj. Gen. Irvin McDowell's thirty-thousand-strong First Corps (detached from the Army of the Potomac) was situated at Fredericksburg. McDowell's corps was sup-posed to march overland, threaten Richmond from the north, and unite with McClellan. However, because Pres. Abraham Lincoln did not think McClellan had left sufficient troops to defend Washington, the First Corps was detached and positioned to cover the southern approach to the city.[25]

The other two Union field forces served under Maj. Gen. John C. Frémont and Maj. Gen. Nathaniel P. Banks. Frémont's 15,000 troops in the newly created Mountain Department were located west of the Shenandoah Moun-tains. Banks commanded 23,000 troops in the Shenandoah Valley.[26]

During Maj. Gen. Thomas J. "Stonewall" Jackson's brilliant Shenandoah Valley Campaign in May and June 1862, an attempt was made to maneuver the forces of McDowell, Frémont, and Banks to trap Jackson. The uncoordinated and inept movements by the commanders of these Union forces made Lincoln and Sec. of War Edwin M. Stanton consider a reorganizational approach.[27]

Born in 1814 in Steubenville, Ohio, Edwin M. Stanton was a lawyer prior to the Civil War. His most famous case was the defense of Daniel E. Sickles, who was charged with the murder of his wife's lover. Stanton first successfully

Sec. of War Edwin M. Stanton, USA.
Library of Congress.

used the insanity defense in this trial. In 1860 he was appointed US attorney general. In January 1862 Lincoln made Stanton secretary of war, a position he held until 1868, when he returned to private law practice. Shortly afterward Stanton was appointed to the Supreme Court, but died in 1869 before taking the oath of office.[28]

Frémont's, Banks's, and McDowell's forces were combined into the Army of Virginia. Frémont's command became the First Corps. When Frémont resigned rather than serve under a junior-ranking officer, Maj. Gen. Franz Sigel replaced him. Banks's command became the Second Corps, and McDowell's corps was redesignated the Third Corps.[29]

Searching for an army commander, Lincoln and Stanton turned to the Western Theater, where one officer seemed to hold promise. John Pope, a Kentuckian, had graduated from West Point in 1842 and served in the Mexican War. He was ordered east and arrived in Washington on June 24. On June 26, 1862, Lincoln signed an order creating the Army of Virginia and appointed forty-year-old Pope its commander.[30]

Pope and his army were assigned three broad objectives: protect Washington, defend the Shenandoah Valley, and disrupt the Virginia Central Railroad in the vicinity of Charlottesville and Gordonsville. In threatening this vital railroad, Federals thought they would compel Lee to draw off part of his army from the defense of Richmond, which would support McClellan's operation. The commands that formed the Army of Virginia required a period of reorganization and resupply. It was not until mid-July that Pope could tentatively commence moving his army into central Virginia.[31]

Options

The decision facing Maj. Gen. Henry W. Halleck, the Union general-in-chief, was what the Army of the Potomac should do now. Halleck had three options to choose from: He could have McClellan resume the offense and maneuver against Lee's army and Richmond. Alternatively, he could send McClellan across the James River to maneuver against Petersburg and the railroad junction there. Finally, Halleck could have the Army of the Potomac evacuate the Virginia Peninsula and return to the Washington-Alexandria area.[32]

Option 1

Remaining north of the James River and maneuvering against Lee's army with the intent of capturing Richmond was a viable option. The Army of the Potomac already occupied a defensible lodgment area at Harrison's Landing and had a secure naval line of supply on the James River. At this location McClellan could resupply his army, then commence another offensive against Richmond, only twenty-five miles away. Lee would have to maneuver and attack or defend against this threat.

Maj. Gen. John Pope, USA. U.S. Army Heritage Education Center.

Pope's army was in central Virginia and moving toward Richmond and the vital railroads from the Shenandoah Valley and other areas in the western Confederacy. Pope would also pose a second threat that the Confederate commander could not ignore. The simultaneous maneuvering by McClellan and Pope against Richmond would present Lee with a difficult tactical situation.

The disadvantage to this option was that both Union armies would have to develop and keep their maneuverings coordinated. If one force stopped or went on the defense, Lee could focus on and attack the other.

Option 2

McClellan could cross his army to the south side of the James River and move toward Petersburg, as Grant would do in 1864.

Richmond and the Army of Northern Virginia were supplied by railroads from the south and from the west. South of Richmond three lines came into Petersburg: the South Side Railroad, the Weldon Railroad, and the Petersburg Railroad. The Richmond and Petersburg Railroad went north from this junction to Richmond. The Virginia Central Railroad and the Richmond and Danville Railroad entered Richmond from the western part of the state. Connected to the southern, central, and western Confederacy by other railroads, these were vital communication and supply lines for the Army of Northern Virginia as well as the Confederate capital.[33]

Capturing Petersburg would sever the railroad supply lines from the south and severely reduce the ability to supply Lee's army and the Confederate capital. Pope's simultaneous capture of any section of the Virginia Central Railroad, leaving only the Richmond and Danville Railroad open, would significantly limit the amount of supplies and equipment coming from the Shenandoah Valley and the western Confederacy.

One rail line would be insufficient to supply the Army of Northern Virginia. Lee could not ignore the threat to or loss of these railroads, and he would be forced to maneuver against one or perhaps both of the Union armies.

If the Federals captured Petersburg McClellan would be able to move directly against Richmond, just twenty miles away. As with Option 1, both Union armies would have to coordinate their movements lest Lee create the opportunity to decisively engage them separately. So far, no Union command structure had demonstrated such coordination capability.

Option 3

Halleck could order McClellan to abandon the campaign, move his army to the Fort Monroe area, and then travel by ship to the Washington-

Alexandria area. Once completed, such a move would place McClellan's and Pope's armies in close proximity to each other. Their combined strength would give the Union commanders a distinct advantage over Lee.[34]

This option had disadvantages. McClellan's army would at times be unable to operate with or reinforce Pope's. The Army of the Potomac's units would be unavailable while at the southern tip of the Peninsula or in transit by ships. This would provide Lee the opportunity to maneuver against and attack Pope's army while it was isolated.

A Union withdrawal from the Peninsula would also give up all the gains Federal forces had made since April and remove the near threat from Richmond. This, in turn, would briefly eliminate the two-army threat confronting Lee. The return of the Army of the Potomac to the Washington-Alexandria area would bring the Union operational situation full circle in Virginia, with the army where it had been in March.

Decision

Supported by Lincoln, Halleck ordered McClellan to move his army to Fort Monroe on the tip of the Virginia Peninsula, and then to return it to the Washington-Alexandria area by ships.

On July 25 Halleck visited McClellan at Harrison's Landing. During this meeting the two generals discussed what McClellan should do next. He favored crossing the James River and moving on Petersburg, but Halleck informed him this was not a favorable option. However, Halleck stated that McClellan would receive twenty thousand troops as reinforcements if he commenced operation against Richmond on the north side of the James River. If McClellan could not do so, then Halleck thought his army should be removed from the Peninsula. Halleck returned to Washington believing McClellan would accept the twenty thousand soldiers and recommence operation north of the river.[35]

After returning to Washington, Halleck received a request from McClellan for a reinforcement of sixty thousand more troops before he could move on Richmond. Halleck's response was to order McClellan to remove his army from the Peninsula and bring it back north by ships.[36]

Results/Impact:

Halleck's critical decision had an immediate and far-reaching impact on events in the Eastern Theater for the remainder of 1862 and beyond. Evacuating the Army of the Potomac ended the prospect of a Union army operating in the vicinity of Richmond until mid-1864.

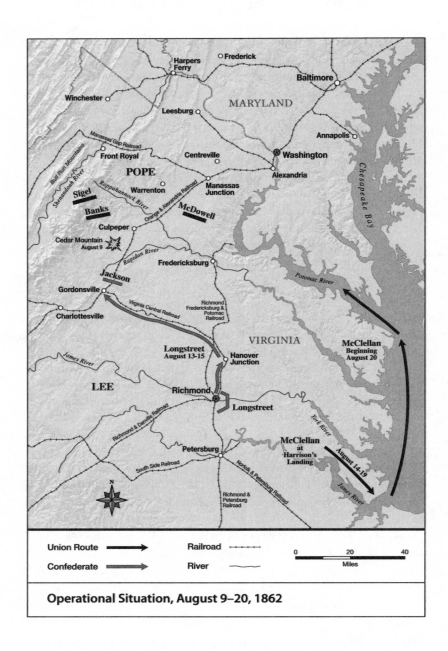

Operational Situation, August 9–20, 1862

Union Route →
Confederate ⇒
Railroad ┝┝┝┝
River ~~~

0   20   40
Miles

With Pope's Army of Virginia moving south through central Virginia and McClellan's army at Harrison's Landing, Lee confronted a dual threat whose combined strength was significantly greater than his. Retreat removed this menace and provided Lee the time to concentrate and maneuver against Pope's army while McClellan's men were en route back to northern Virginia. This led to a Confederate victory at the Second Battle of Manassas, which in turn set the stage for Lee's incursion into Maryland. Lee was stopped along Antietam Creek, and he then retreated back to Virginia. Lincoln subsequently issued the Emancipation Proclamation, which eventually changed the character and goals of the entire war.

CHAPTER 5

SUMMARY AND AFTERWARD

Summary

Although many important decisions were made prior to, during, and just after the Seven Days Battles, only sixteen of them were critical decisions. These decisions were of such magnitude as to affect the events immediately following them and shape the course of events from that point on. Ultimately, they determined the battles and operational maneuvering as we know it today. Of the sixteen critical decisions of the Seven Days, three were strategic, four were operational, eight were tactical, and one was personnel. Viewing the decisions from the levels of command, there were four national-level decisions, one wing/corps-level decision, nine army-level decisions, and two division-level decisions. Seven of the critical decisions were made by a Union commander and nine were made by a Confederate commander.

McClellan Decides on a Turning Movement—
Army-Level Strategic Decision

This decision initiated a series of events that led to the Seven Days' Battles. Although Maj. Gen. George B. McClellan had taken command of the Army of the Potomac in August 1861, his soldiers had engaged in no significant activity as the campaign season slipped into winter. Under pressure to begin operations in the spring of 1862, McClellan developed a plan to use Union sea power to move his army to Urbana. However, this plan became unviable in March when Confederate forces commanded by Gen. Joseph E. Johnston retreated south thirty-six miles from the vicinity of Centreville to the Rappahannock River. McClellan then modified his plan and moved his army to Fort Monroe on the tip of the Peninsula. In so doing, he moved the center of the war in the East from outside of Washington to a location where the Confederate capital was threatened and might be captured before sufficient rebel forces could be redeployed for its defense. The series of events set in motion by this decision led to the Seven Days' Battles.

McClellan Decides on a Siege at Yorktown—
Army-Level Tactical Decision

The Army of the Potomac commenced departing from Alexandria, Virginia, on March 17 by navy and civilian ships. By April McClellan had sufficient manpower at Fort Monroe (approximately fifty thousand men), with more soldiers arriving every day, to begin operations and move against the Confederate position at Yorktown and along a line across the Peninsula. The Confederate force, approximately thirteen thousand troops, was commanded by Maj. Gen. John B. Magruder. Magruder used his soldiers to bluff McClellan into thinking he had a significantly larger force. Rather than attack, the Union commander decided to lay siege to the Yorktown defenses. Moving forward and emplacing the siege artillery took Federal troops from mid-April to May 2. This delay afforded Johnston time to move a significant portion of his army from the Rappahannock River line to the southern part of the Peninsula. The Confederates abandoned their position at Yorktown the night before McClellan began his siege. As a result of this decision, McClellan lost the operational advantage he had gained by moving to the Peninsula. Enough Confederate forces were deployed between his army and Richmond to close his once-open road to the capital.

McDowell Is Diverted—National-Level
Operational Decision

Before Maj. Gen. Irvin McDowell's First Corps could be transferred to the Virginia Peninsula, Lincoln held it back and positioned it to defend Washington. When Johnston moved his army from the Rappahannock River line to the Peninsula, McDowell's corps moved farther south to just across the Rappahannock from Fredericksburg. In mid-May McDowell was ordered to move farther south toward Richmond. However, a few days later Maj. Gen. Thomas J. "Stonewall" Jackson began his Valley Campaign. In an attempt to cut Jackson off while he was in the northern Shenandoah Valley, McDowell's corps, in conjunction with two other commands, was ordered to concentrate near Strasburg. This attempt was unsuccessful, and a large portion of McDowell's troops spent time marching to the valley and then back to Fredericksburg. As a result of this decision, McDowell's large corps (33,510 troops) did not join the Army of the Potomac on that army's right flank. Such a juncture would have extended the Union lines at Richmond to the north and west. Furthermore, this position would have precluded the turning movement Lee planned against McClellan's right rear area and supply line and base. It would have also blocked Jackson from joining Lee as he did in late June.

Davis Decides on Lee—National-Level Personnel Decision

After abandoning the Yorktown defenses, Johnston conducted a delay and withdrew up the Peninsula. On May 31 he attacked a portion of the Union army at Seven Pines (Fair Oaks), and he was severely wounded and evacuated during the battle. Jefferson Davis needed to appoint a new army commander in Johnston's place. He had several options as to whom that officer would be, but in the end the Confederate president decided on Gen. Robert E. Lee. On June 1 Lee was appointed the commander of the Army of Northern Virginia. This far reaching decision not only led to the Seven Days Battles, but also determined how the war would be fought in the Eastern Theater for the rest of the conflict.

Jackson Wants to Invade—National-Level Strategic Decision

Upon the completion of his Valley Campaign, Jackson was located in the southern Shenandoah Valley. He proposed that if his command could be reinforced to a strength of 40,000 troops, he could move north and cross into Maryland and Pennsylvania. As Jackson had 16,000 troops, he would require 24,000 more. Approximately 16,500 soldiers could be sent to him, bringing his total force to 32,500 and leaving a shortfall of 7,500. If he could move north with this strength, Jackson would have a major impact on the war in the East. McClellan would probably have to withdraw part of his army from in front of Richmond and send the soldiers back to northern Virginia, which would impact his operations. Lee would not have sufficient troops available to execute the turning movement he was planning. Thus there would be no Seven Days Battles. Facing two options, Davis decided Jackson would not invade, which made his command available for Lee to use in the Seven Days.

Lee Decides on a Turning Movement—
Army-Level Operational Decision

When Lee assumed command of the Army of Northern Virginia, it was located on the eastern edge of Richmond and besieged by a larger Union army. Lee knew that McClellan would conduct a siege operation against him and eventually overcome his defensive positions. To counter this Union capability, he planned a turning movement around McClellan's right (north) flank. This offensive operation would move Confederate forces deep into the Union right rear area and threaten the supply line and the major supply base at White House Landing. These threats would turn McClellan's position and force him to reorient toward Lee's threat, in turn leading to a battle of maneuver. Lee's offensive concept would initiate the Seven Days Battles.

A. P. Hill Attacks—Division-Level Tactical Decision

Lee's plan for a turning movement was for part of his army to hold a positon in front of Richmond while three divisions were located farther to the left (north). These divisions would join with Jackson's command after it moved from the Shenandoah Valley to Ashland, then south toward the Union right rear area. A. P. Hill's Division was the leftmost of these three units. When Hill made contact with Jackson, he was to cross the Chickahominy River and move south to Mechanicsville. This move would support Jackson and also clear the way for the other two divisions to cross the Chickahominy. However, Jackson failed to reach his attack position on June 26, and A. P. Hill decided to attack across the river anyway. These events initiated the first battle of the Seven Days with Hill's men and two other divisions. Without Jackson, Lee's plan did not develop as he intended. However, Lee did take the initiative away from McClellan and upset any future plans.

McClellan Provides Minimal Reinforcements—
Army-Level Tactical Decision

Despite the successful defense by Brig. Gen. Fitz John Porter's Fifth Corps at Mechanicsville, on the night of June 26 McClellan ordered him to abandon the position. Porter's corps withdrew to the east and established a strong position overlooking Boatswain's Swamp. Lee continued to attempt his turning movement, but he came up against Porter's new location. Throughout June 27, Lee committed all six divisions of his maneuver force in attacks against the defenders in the Battle of Gaines' Mill. This course of action provided McClellan the opportunity to fight a potentially decisive defensive battle and even counterattack the left (east) flank of Lee's army. To do so would require that significant reinforcement be sent north across the Chickahominy River. McClellan decided not to dispatch troops for this purpose. Late in the afternoon he provided only minimum reinforcements that covered the retreat of the Fifth Corps after it was forced from its position. Having lost the tactical initiative to Lee, McClellan failed to use this opportunity to regain the initiative. He would never regain the initiative for the remainder of the Seven Days.

McClellan Decides to Retreat to the James River— Army-Level Operational Decision

After the Battle of Gaines' Mill, McClellan's army was concentrated on the south side of the Chickahominy River. The Federal commander could hold Lee along the line of the river and attack, with the remainder of his army, the force covering Richmond. Such an operation would probably have been successful, McClellan instead decided to retreat to the James River. There, he could reestablish a supply base, use the river as a line of communication, and be supported by the navy's gunboats. With this decision McClellan gave up any thoughts or pretentions of capturing Richmond. For the Army of the Potomac, the Seven Days turned into a series of successful defensive battles followed by retreats.

Lee Decides on a Pursuit—Army-Level Operational Decision

When Porter's corps retreated across the Chickahominy River, Lee temporarily lost contact with the Union force in front of him. It required twenty-four hours for Lee to determine that McClellan was retreating south across and not east down the Peninsula. The rebel general had not given up on seriously damaging or destroying the Army of the Potomac. To accomplish this objective, he decided on a pursuit. Jackson's and Magruder's Commands were to apply direct pressure to the rear guard of the Union army in an attempt to slow its retreat. Longstreet, A. P. Hill, and Huger would march to obtain a position at Glendale to cut the route of retreat. If successful, this plan would block all or a major portion of McClellan's army from the James River and force a decisive battle. Lee's decision continued combat operations for three more days.

Jackson Decides Not to Cross White Oak Swamp— Wing/Corps-Level Tactical Decision

As part of the pursuit, Jackson's Command was a direct pressure force that was to maintain close contact with the retreating Union army. It was also charged with attacking and attempting to slow down the withdrawal whenever the opportunity presented itself. Jackson's planned route after crossing the Chickahominy extended south, crossed White Oak Swamp, proceeded on to Glendale, and then eventually to Malvern Hill. However, when Jackson reached White Oak Swamp, he found a Union force on the other (south) side barring his way. Rather than aggressively maneuver and attack, he allowed his command to sit mostly idle on the northern edge of the swamp. Jackson's decision kept him out of the fight at Glendale, where his command could have had a positive effect on the battle. In addition, his choice allowed Union troops at White Oak Swamp to be sent as reinforcement to the Glendale fight. The result was a nullification of a major portion of Lee's plan, and it would contribute to the Union army's survival at Glendale, followed by a repositioning to Malvern Hill.

Huger Decides Not to Attack—Division-Level Tactical Decision

As part of Lee's plan, Maj. Gen. Benjamin Huger's division was to march down the Charles City Road and, in conjunction with Longstreet's and A. P. Hill's Divisions, attack the Union forces at the Glendale Crossroads on June 30. That morning Huger's Division was three miles from the crossroads. A mile after it commenced moving, the force encountered a wooded area with felled trees blocking the road. Although the trees were an obstacle to artillery and wagons, infantry could continue toward Glendale with difficulty. Huger, however, decided that he would cut a parallel road through the woods rather than clear the road or just proceed with his infantry. Union troops were able to continue felling trees as fast as Confederates cut the new route. As a result, Lee found another segment of his plan neutralized, and Huger's Division did not arrive at Glendale in time to have any effect on the battle. Huger's decision along with Jackson's keep four badly needed divisions out of the fight at the Glendale Crossroads. This greatly contributed to the Union troops' success at Glendale and their eventual retreat to Malvern Hill.

Magruder Is Ordered to Support Holmes— Army-Level Tactical Decision

As part of Lee's plan, Maj. Gen. John B. Magruder was order to follow Longstreet and A. P. Hill and be prepared to support them. On June 30 Lee received a report that Union wagons were crossing over Malvern Hill. He then ordered Maj. Gen. Theophilus H. Holmes, whose division was on the River Road, to employ artillery and infantry against the US forces on the hill. The Union position was stronger than Lee realized, and Holmes was unsuccessful.

Lee then directed Magruder's Division, essentially the army's only reserve, to stop following Longstreet and A. P. Hill and move south to support Holmes. Longstreet and A. P. Hill commenced their attacks at Glendale shortly thereafter. Several hours later, Magruder was ordered to reverse course and march to Glendale. By the time his troops got there, it was too late. Lee's decision removed another division from his attack and together with Jackson's and Huger's four divisions resulted in a major portion of Lee's army (five divisions with 17 infantry brigades and 23 artillery batteries) not getting into action. It allowed a successful Union defense followed by a march to Malvern Hill.

Lee Orders an Attack—Army-Level Tactical Decision

On July 1 the Army of the Potomac had formed a formidable artillery and infantry defensive position on Malvern Hill. Confederate divisions began to move within striking distance of the Union defenses in the morning and early afternoon. When Union artillery defeated planned cross fire of Confederate artillery, it appeared that no infantry assault would take place. However, when Lee received incorrect information that Union artillery and infantry were withdrawing, he ordered his infantry to attack. This action resulted in multiple unsuccessful brigade attacks, a high casualty rate, and a major Union victory. Malvern Hill was Lee's last chance to severely damage McClellan's army. For Confederates, this battle with 5,650 casualties was the second-bloodiest engagement of the Seven Days. With other Seven Days Battles, Lee's force had sustained 20,204 casualties, or 22 percent of its strength. A review of the past seven days would lead Lee to cease combat operation and begin to consolidate, reorganize, and resupply his army.

McClellan Retreats Again—Army-Level Tactical Decision

McClellan had won a resounding defensive victory on July 1. He now had the opportunity to hold his strong position or counterattack, and he chose to do neither. On the night of July 1, Union troops abandoned the Malvern Hill position and continued their retreat. On July 2 and 3 McClellan's army marched on the River Road to Berkley Plantation and Harrison's Landing. With this decision the Federal commander gave up any tactical advantages he had gained on July 1 and essentially ended the Seven Days Battles.

Halleck Decides to Evacuate the Peninsula— National-Level Strategic Decision

The Army of the Potomac occupied positions at Berkley Plantation and Harrison's Landing from July 3 onward into August. This was a time of defense and resupply, as no offensive operations were conducted. McClellan was visited by Lincoln and then by the new general-in-chief, Maj. Gen. Henry W. Halleck. Halleck and McClellan discussed several offensive options, but when McClellan began demanding more troops and stalling, Halleck ordered the Army of the Potomac to march to Fort Monroe and return to Alexandria and Washington by ships. This decision ended combat operations on the Virginia Peninsula. Union troops would not be this close to Richmond until the late summer of 1864.

Afterward

Union victories in the first half of 1862 gave Northerners hope that the war would soon conclude with victory and the seceding Southern states' return to the United States. In February Brig. Gen. Ulysses S. Grant had captured Forts Henry and Donelson and opened the Cumberland and Tennessee Rivers to Nashville and Muscle Shoals, Alabama. These actions had broken the Confederate defensive line in the Western Theater, which stretched from the mountains across Kentucky and Tennessee to the Mississippi River. In early April, Grant's and Maj. Gen. Don Carlos Buell's armies defeated Gen. Albert S. Johnston's Confederate army at the Battle of Shiloh. In June, Federals captured Corinth, Mississippi, with its strategic railroad junction. In the meantime, Rear Adm. David G. Farragut seized New Orleans, the South's largest city, in late April.

In the Eastern Theater, Maj. Gen. George B. McClellan moved his army to the southern tip of the Virginia Peninsula in March and began a slow campaign of maneuver designed to capture Richmond, the Confederate capital. At the end of May, the Army of the Potomac was located on the eastern edge of Richmond. On June 2 Gen. Robert E. Lee was appointed commander of the Army of Northern Virginia, and in the last week of that month he launched the Seven Days Battles, changing everything. Lee was unable to trap and destroy McClellan's army, but he did drive it away from Richmond to a position on the James River. The Federals evacuated back to Alexandria and Washington in August.

In the meantime, Lee shifted his army northward and defeated the newly created Union Army of Virginia, commanded by Maj. Gen. John Pope, at the Second Battle of Manassas. This late August victory and the evacuation of the Army of the Potomac shifted the center of the war in Virginia from just outside of Richmond to the western approaches to Washington, DC. Lee followed these actions with an incursion into Maryland that ended at the Battle of Antietam on September 17. Moving back into Virginia, the Union and Confederate armies fought at Fredericksburg in mid-December. This was a spectacular Confederate victory, and in the East, it completed the reversal of Union good fortunes that had begun ten months earlier.

In the Western Theater, Confederate defeats had been partially reversed when Maj. Gen. Kirby Smith's and Gen. Braxton Bragg's armies invaded Kentucky. Although a Union victory at Perryville on October 8 forced a rebel retreat, much of central and Eastern Tennessee had been returned to Confederate control. In the last month of the year, Grant began his land campaign to capture Vicksburg. His troops turned back when his supply base at Holly Springs was destroyed. At the end of the year, the Union military had only one bright light—the Army of the Cumberland, led by Maj. Gen. William S. Rosecrans, declared victory over Bragg's Army of Tennessee at Stones River in north-central Tennessee.

This period of time also became a watershed in the Civil War. Initial thought on both sides was that the conflict would be short and yield relatively few casualties. In the first half of the year, the Battle of Shiloh ended with 23,741 casualties (13,047 Union and 10,694 Confederate), and the Seven Days Battles resulted in 35,999 casualties (15,795 Union and 20,204 Confederate) almost three months later. These 59,740 casualties from just two engagements were a harbinger of what was to come—a much longer and costlier war than had been imagined.

Casualties for the remainder of 1862 reinforced the length and costliness of the conflict: Second Manassas, 26,551 (17,354 Union and 9,197 Confederate); Antietam, 26,134 (12,410 Union and 13,724 Confederate); Perryville, 7,607 (4,211 Union and 3,396 Confederate); Fredericksburg, 18,000 (12,700 Union and 5,300 Confederate); and Stones River, 23,515 (13,249 Union and 10,266 Confederate). Casualties from major battles in 1862 totaled 161,547 (88,766 Union and 72,781 Confederate). This number was approximately 84 percent of the combined strength of the Army of the Potomac and Army of Northern Virginia in June 1862.[1]

As foretold, it was to be a long and bloody war.

APPENDIX I

BATTLEFIELD GUIDE TO THE DECISIONS OF THE SEVEN DAYS

There is value in being close to or at the place where a critical decision was made or carried out. Insomuch as modern construction allows, seeing the terrain as those who made and executed these decisions did offers a perspective that reading or studying a map cannot. This appendix provides a tour that will place you on the ground as near as possible to the locations where critical decisions were made and carried out.

The tour traces the critical decisions of the Seven Days in chronological order. Driving and walking instructions will guide you to the various locations. Orientating information is provided for each stop, including which direction to face, what units were in your vicinity, the critical decision itself, and its resulting action and impact. Whenever possible, primary source material allows the battles' participants to tell you what happened. Some words in the primary material are spelled differently than they are today, but they have been left as written by the battles' participants. If you need more information, read the critical-decision discussion in the appropriate chapter.

The Seven Days battles were fluid, some involving considerable movement. When looking at the maps in this appendix you must therefore remember they present a brief snapshot of many unit movements. The maps are designed to be a frame of reference that will allow you to visualize the events that transpired as you read accounts of the fighting.

A majority of the critical decisions were made within the confines of the various battlefields. However, six of these decisions were made somewhere else, and it is not practical to include them as stops. Those critical decisions were as follows: McClellan Decides on a Turning Movement, McClellan Decides on a Siege at Yorktown, McDowell Is Diverted, Davis Decides on Lee, Jackson Wants to Invade, and Halleck Decides to Evacuate the Peninsula.

Driving north or south on I-295, take Exit 31B onto North Airport Drive (Highway 156) to Highland Springs. Drive west on North Airport Drive for 1.8 mile to the intersection with Nine Mile Road (Highway 33). Turn right onto Nine Mile Road and drive north, then west for 4.0 miles. After you cross Dabbs House Road, look for County of Henrico and Dabbs House Museum signs, turn right, and drive to the parking area for the Dabbs House.

Alternate: Traveling on I-64 North or I-64 South, take Exit 194B onto Nine Mile Road (Highway 33). Drive east on Nine Mile Road (Highway 33) for 0.4 mile to the County of Henrico and Dabbs House Museum signs, turn left, and drive to the parking area for the Dabbs House. You may wish to visit the museum.

Stop 1—Lee's Headquarters

In June this house was Lee's headquarters. It was here on June 23, 1862, that he met with Jackson, Longstreet, A. P. Hill, and D. H. Hill to give them his order that would begin the Seven Days. Lee then left the meeting for a period of time so the other four could work out the details. One of the officers' decisions was that Jackson would have his command in position for the turning movement by 3:00 a.m. on June 26.

Narrative of Maj. Gen. James Longstreet, CSA, Commanding Longstreet's Division, Army of Northern Virginia

Jackson was called in advance of command to meet the Hills and myself at General Lee's headquarters for a conference on the execution. On the forenoon of the 23d of June we were advised of his approach, and called to headquarters to meet him. He was there before us, having ridden fifty miles by relay of horses since midnight. We were together in a few minutes after his arrival, in General Lee's private office. The general [Lee] explained the plan briefly: Jackson to march from Ashland by the heights between the Chickahominy and Pamunkey [Rivers], turning and dislodging the Federal right, thus clearing the way for the march of troops on his right; A. P. Hill to cross the upper Chickahominy and march for Mechanicsville, in echelon to Jackson; the Mechanicsville Bridge being clear, D. H. Hill's Division and mine to cross, the former to reinforce Jackson's column, the latter to file to the right and march down the [Chickahominy] river in right echelon to A. P. Hill's direct march through Mechanicville to Gaines's Mill.

General Lee then excused himself to attend to office business, asking that we talk the matter over for our better comprehension.

Turning to Jackson, I said,—

"You have distance to overcome, and in all probability, obstacles will be thrown in the way of your march by the enemy. As your move is the key of the campaign, you should appoint the hour at which the connection may be made co-operative."

He promptly responded,—

"The morning of the 25th."

I expressed doubt of his meeting that hour, and suggested that it would be better to take a little more time, as the movement of our columns could be readily adjusted to those of his. He then appointed the morning of the 26th.

Upon his return, report was made to General Lee that the officers understood, and would be prepared to execute the plans; that General Jackson had appointed the morning of the 26th, when he would lead the march [attack]. Verbal instructions were given, followed by written orders, embodying in minute detail the plans already given in general.[1]

Return to your car for the drive to Stop 2. Depart the Dabbs House and return to Nine Mile Road (Highway 33). Turn right onto Nine Mile Road and drive 0.4 mile to I-64. Take the right access to I-64. Drive north on I-64 for 0.9 mile to Exit 192 to the Mechanicsville Turnpike (Highway 360). Exit to the right, then turn right onto the Mechanicsville Turnpike. Drive northeast on the Mechanicsville Turnpike for 1.9 mile to the National Park sign "Chickahominy Bluff, Richmond National Battlefield Park." Just before the sign, turn right onto the park road and drive to the parking area. Park, leave your car and walk to where the fence protects the earthworks.

Stop 2—Chickahominy Bluffs

The earthworks are the remains of some of the defensive positions Lee had constructed east and northeast of Richmond. They were designed to allow his army to maintain a reduced presence in front of the Union force while he shifted troops for an attack and turning movement against McClellan's right (north) flank.

D. H. Hill's and Longstreet's Divisions were deployed where you are. Both were to use the Mechanicsville Turnpike and bridge to cross the Chickahominy River. The turnpike is 100 yards to your left; you drove on it to this position. The bridge and river are 1,400 yards (0.8 mile) in front of you. A. P. Hill's Division was positioned 3,700 yards (2.1 miles) to your left (northwest). General Orders No. 75 was Lee's order for the turning movement.

GENERAL ORDERS No. 75
HDQRS. ARMY OF NORTHERN VIRGINIA,
June 24, 1862

I. General Jackson's command will proceed to-morrow from Ashland toward the Slash Church and encamp at some convenient point west of the Central Railroad. Branch's brigade, of A. P. Hill's division, will also to-morrow evening take position on the Chickahominy near Half. Sink. At 3 o'clock Thursday morning, 26th instant, General Jackson will advance on the road leading to Pole Green Church, communicating his march to General Branch, who will immediately cross the Chickahominy and take the road leading to Mechanicsville. As soon as the movements of these columns are discovered, General A. P. Hill, with the rest of his division, will cross the Chickahominy near Meadow Bridge and move direct upon Mechanicsville. To aid his advance, the heavy batteries on the Chickahominy will at the proper time open upon the batteries at Mechanicsville. The enemy being driven from Mechanicsville and the passage across the bridge opened, General Longstreet, with his division and that of General D. H. Hill, will cross the Chickahominy at or near that point, General D. H. Hill moving to the support of General Jackson and General Longstreet supporting General A. P. Hill. The [two] divisions, keeping in communication with each other and moving *en échelon* on separate roads, if practicable, the left division in advance, with skirmishers and sharpshooters extending their front, will sweep down the Chickahominy and endeavor to drive the enemy from his position above New Bridge, General Jackson bearing well to his left, turning Beaver Dam Creek and taking the direction toward Cold Harbor. They will then press forward toward the York River Railroad, closing upon the enemy's rear and forcing him down the Chickahominy. Any advance of the enemy toward Richmond will be prevented by vigorously following his rear and crippling and arresting his progress.

II. The divisions under Generals Huger and Magruder will hold their positions in front of the enemy against attack, and make such demonstrations Thursday as to discover his operations. Should opportunity offer, the feint will be converted into a real attack, and should an abandonment of his intrenchments by the enemy be discovered, he will be closely pursued.

III. The Third Virginia Cavalry will observe the Charles City road. The Fifth Virginia, the First North Carolina, and the Hampton Legion (cavalry) will observe the Darbytown, Varina, and Osborne roads. Should a movement of the enemy down the Chickahominy be discovered, they will close upon his flank and endeavor to arrest his march.

IV. General Stuart, with the First, Fourth, and Ninth Virginia Cavalry, the cavalry of Cobb's Legion and the Jeff. Davis Legion, will cross the Chickahominy to-morrow and take position to the left of General Jackson's line of march. The main body will be held in reserve, with scouts well extended to the front and left. General Stuart will keep General Jackson informed of the movements of the enemy on his left and will co-operate with him in his advance. The Tenth Virginia Cavalry, Colonel Davis, will remain on the Nine-mile road.

V. General Ransom's brigade, of General Holmes' command, will be placed in reserve on the Williamsburg road by General Huger, to whom he will report for orders.

VI. Commanders of divisions will cause their commands to be provided with three days' cooked rations. The necessary ambulances and ordnance trains will be ready to accompany the divisions and receive orders from their respective commanders. Officers in charge of all trains will invariably remain with them. Batteries and wagons will keep on the right of the road. The chief engineer, Major Stevens, will assign engineer officers to each division, whose duty it will be to make provision for overcoming all difficulties to the progress of the troops. The staff departments will give the necessary instructions to facilitate the movements herein directed.

By command of General Lee:
R. H. CHILTON, Assistant Adjutant-General.[2]

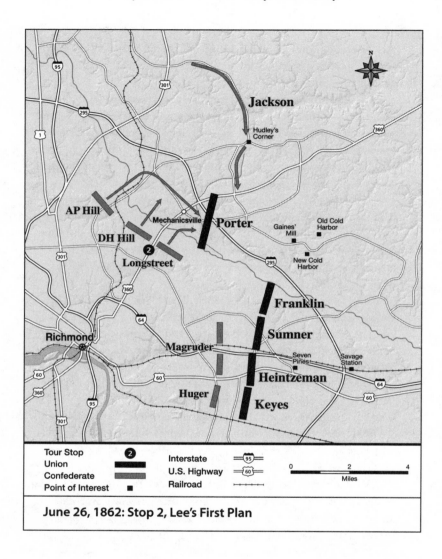

June 26, 1862: Stop 2, Lee's First Plan

Lee was in this vicinity awaiting A. P. Hill's assault, which would mean Jackson had made it to his attack position farther to the north and was in the process of turning the Union right.

Return to your car. Drive back to the Mechanicsville Turnpike (Highway 360). Make a left turn onto the Mechanicsville Turnpike, and drive southwest for 0.4 mile to the intersection with East Laburnum Avenue. Turn right onto East Laburnum Avenue, and drive northwest for 1.6 miles to the

Richmond-Henrico Turnpike (Highway 627). Turn right onto the Richmond-Henrico Turnpike and drive north, then northeast for 1.9 miles. Pull off to the side of the road just after you cross the railroad tracks at the end of this 1.9-mile segment. You will see a historical placard to your left directly across the road. Be careful of traffic, get out of your car, and look in the direction you were driving.

Stop 3—Meadow Bridge, A. P. Hill Decides to Attack

Meadow Bridge and the Chickahominy are approximately 0.4 mile in front of you. This is the position of A. P. Hill's Division. The division was formed in a column of brigades with Brig. Gen. Charles W. Field's brigade in the lead and at this location.

Jackson's column was running way behind schedule. Brig. Gen. Lawrence Branch, positioned north of his division, was to inform A. P. Hill when contact was made with Jackson. Branch made contact with Jackson's column, but he did not inform A. P. Hill, and he failed to relay Jackson's lateness or his location. Neither A. P. Hill or Branch communicated with each other. Although A. P. Hill and Lee were only 2.1 miles apart, they also did not communicate. Late in the afternoon and on his own, A. P. Hill made the critical decision for his division to cross the Chickahominy River and commence its attack. This choice put the left wing of Lee's army into motion without Jackson being in position. A. P. Hill's movement brought his division into frontal assaults against the Union's strong position at Beaver Dam Creek.

Report of Maj. Gen. Ambrose P. Hill, CSA, Commanding A. P. Hill's Division, Army of Northern Virginia

In obedience to orders, received from the general commanding, on Wednesday night, June 25, I concentrated my division near the Meadow Bridge, viz: The brigades of J. R. Anderson, Gregg, Field, Pender, and Archer, the brigade of General Branch having been directed to move to the bridge some 7 miles above, where the Brooke turnpike crosses the Chickahominy, the batteries of Braxton, Andrews, Pegram, Crenshaw, Mcintosh, Bachman, and Johnson, with four extra horses to each gun (Johnson's battery accompanied Branch), in all about 14,000 men. The brigades and batteries were entirely concealed from the view of the enemy.

My orders were that General Jackson, moving down from Ashland, would inform General Branch of his near approach. As soon as

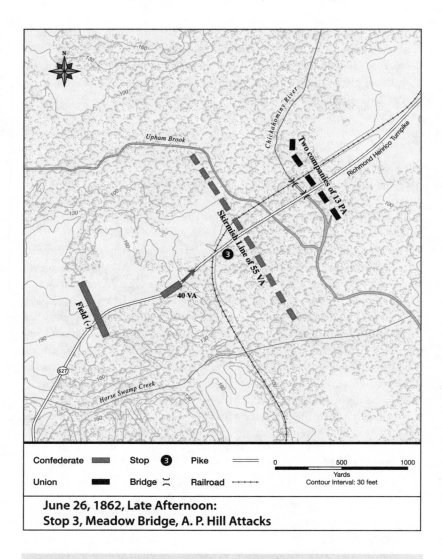

Confederate � Stop ❸ Pike ═══ 0 500 1000

Union ▬ Bridge ⌣ Railroad ┼─┼─┼

Yards

Contour Interval: 30 feet

June 26, 1862, Late Afternoon:
Stop 3, Meadow Bridge, A. P. Hill Attacks

Jackson crossed the Central Railroad Branch was to cross the Chickahominy, and, taking the river road, push on and clear the Meadow Bridge. This done, I was to cross at Meadow Bridge, and, sweeping down to Mechanicsville, open the way for General Longstreet. It was expected that General Jackson would be in the position assigned him by early dawn, and all my preparations were made with the view of moving early. General Branch, however, did not receive intelligence from General Jackson until about 10 o'clock, when he immediately crossed and proceeded to carry out his instructions. He was delayed by the enemy's skirmishers and advanced but slowly.

Three o'clock having arrived, and no intelligence from Jackson or Branch, I determined to cross at once rather than hazard the failure of the whole plan by longer deferring it. General Field, already selected for the advance, being in readiness, seized the bridge, and the Fortieth Virginia, Colonel Brockenbrough, leading, his brigade passed over, meeting but slight opposition, the enemy falling back to Mechanicsville. The division being safely over, Anderson and Archer followed Field; Gregg and Pender turned short to the right, and moved through the fields to co-operate on the right of the first column.[3]

Return to your car. The drive to Stop 4 will follow A. P. Hill's Division as it moved toward Mechanicsville, then deployed to attack the Union position at Beaver Dam Creek. Continue driving on the Richmond-Henrico Turnpike for 1.6 mile to Atlee Road. Turn right onto Atlee Road and drive for 1.6 mile to the intersection with the Mechanicsville Turnpike, where there is a stoplight and the Atlee Road becomes the Cold Harbor Road (Highway 156). Continue through this intersection and drive for 0.8 mile, at which point there will be a road to the right that goes to Beaver Dam Creek. Just before the bridge, look for a "Virginia Civil War Trails" sign with an arrow pointing to the right. Before the intersection with the park road, pull to the side and stop. Get out of your car and position yourself so you can see the bridge and the ground on either side of Beaver Dam Creek. **Be careful of traffic.**

Stop 4—Beaver Dam Creek

Beaver Dam Creek is directly in front of you. The road and bridge were not there in 1862. Instead, the road made a right turn where you currently are, extended south for about 0.3 mile, then turned left, where it crossed Beaver Dam Creek. After it crossed the creek it went through the Union defensive position then turned left and came back out to join this road on the other side of the modern bridge, about where you see the road coming from the right. The road in front of you removed this U-shaped wandering route. Although there were woods to your left and behind you, in 1862 much of the terrain was open and provided good fields of fire and observation.

Union forces in a defensive position on the other side of the creek were Brig. Gen. George A. McCall's three-brigade Pennsylvania Reserves Division of Brig. Gen. Fitz John Porter's Fifth Corps. McCall's division was deployed from the north side of today's Highway 360, to your left, in a southern direction (your right) for about 3,100 yards. Brig. Gen. John F. Reynolds held the right of McCall's line. This brigades right flank (north) flank was north of today's Highway 360. Reynolds's line extended south to just north of where the millpond was in 1862. This is to your left front. Brig. Gen. Truman Seymour's brigade was to Porter's left. Seymour's brigade was astride the historic Old Cold Harbor as it climbed up onto the high ground east of the creek. Supporting artillery, with good fields of fire, was employed with the defending infantry. Brig. Gen. George G. Meade's brigade was the division's reserve and was positioned behind the center of the position. Porter's other two divisions were positioned in depth behind McCall's and to the right rear to protect the right flank.

Report of Brig. Gen. George A. McCall, USA, Commanding Third Division, Fifth Corps, Army of the Potomac

I directed the First and Third Brigades, commanded respectively by Brig. Gens. J. F. Reynolds and T. Seymour, to proceed to Beaver Dam Creek, 1 mile this side of Mechanicsville, and occupy a strong position on its left bank near its junction with the Chickahominy, and thence to throw forward to the heights in front of Mechanicsville one regiment and a battery to relieve Taylor, and to post a strong line of pickets from the Mechanicsville Bridge to the Meadow Bridge. The position selected on the Beaver Dam Creek was naturally a strong one, the left resting on the Chickahominy and the right extending to thick woods beyond the upper Mechanicsville road, which were occupied. The passage of the Beaver Dam Creek was difficult throughout the greater part of my front, and, with the exception of the roads crossing at Ellison's Mill and that above mentioned, impracticable for artillery. On the right of the last-named road an epaulement calculated for four pieces of field artillery was thrown up and rifle pits for a regiment each were constructed in advance of each brigade. Cooper's battery of six 10-pounder Parrott guns on the right of the upper road and Smead's battery (regular) of four 12-pounder guns on the left commanded that approach. De Hart's battery (regular) of six 12-pounder guns was near the front-center, commanding a more distant view of the same road and also the lower road direct to Mechanicsville. I held in reserve the Second Brigade (Meade's) in front of Gaines' farm, ready to act either in support of Reynolds and

Seymour or to oppose the crossing at New Bridge should the enemy attempt it.

In this position I awaited any movements the enemy might initiate.

The enemy was discovered to be in motion and our pickets at Meadow Bridge were driven in by the advancing column of the enemy, and those along the road were ordered to fall back. Soon afterward, when the head of his column approached, my infantry and artillery in front of Mechanicsville were recalled. I now ordered forward Meade's brigade, and directed them to occupy ground in rear of the line, where they would be out of the range of musketry and at a practicable distance for support of any part of the field.[4]

Lee did not plan for A. P. Hill's Division to attack the Federal positions at Beaver Dam Creek. Jackson's turning movement around and behind Porter's right flank would cause the Fifth Corps to retreat or risk being cut off. However, Jackson was late and A. P. Hill crossed the river and was committed to frontal attacks against a strong Union defensive position.

Hill's Division deployed with Pender's Brigade to your right and Field's, Archer's, and Anderson's Brigades, in that order, to your left. These four brigades, later reinforced by Ripley's Brigade of D. H. Hill's Division, made frontal attacks against McCall's position. All the assaults were repulsed, some with high casualties.

Brig. Gen. Charles W Field's brigade attack over the ground to your left, just across the road.

Report of Brig. Gen. Charles W. Field, CSA, Commanding, Field's Brigade, A. P. Hill's Division, Army of Northern Virginia

An active and vigorous fire was opened on us from the batteries situated on the north[east] side of Beaver Dam Creek. I changed front to the left by throwing forward the right wing, and advanced to attack them, directing Captain Pegram to take position and open fire on the enemy's batteries, a part of General Archer's brigade having been ordered by General Hill to support me.

About a mile of open ground was to be gotten over, most of which was swept by three or four batteries, but the brigade in the original order gallantly moved forward, though their ranks were momentarily thinned by the most destructive cannonading I have yet known. Our only safety from this fire lay in pushing forward as rapidly as possible and getting so close to the enemy's infantry as to draw the fire upon his own troops should it be continued. He occupied a wooded hill-side overlooking Beaver Dam Creek. Gaining a dense thicket on this side, the stream only separating us, both sides opened with the musket and continued it until about 9 o'clock at night.[5]

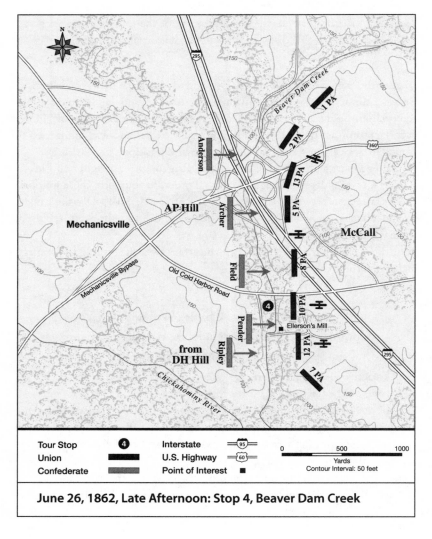

June 26, 1862, Late Afternoon: Stop 4, Beaver Dam Creek

Return to your car. Drive south down the road that goes to the right from Old Cold Harbor Road for 0.2 mile to the parking area, park, get out of your car, and walk to the bridge.

Stop 5—Ellerson's Mill

The 1862 route to Cold Harbor consisted of the road you drove down, then walked on, as well as the bridge crossing Beaver Dam Creek. At the time of the Seven Days, the area was open terrain with good fields of fire. Ellerson's Mill was to your left front as you walk on the bridge. The dirt and gravel road leading away from the bridge was the continuation of the historic Cold Harbor Road in 1862. After crossing the creek, the road proceeded up to the higher ground. There, it turned left and extended to where the modern road is today.

The left (south) part of McCall's defensive position was situated about 125 yards in front of you on the higher ground. From there, the Union position, on the other side of the creek, went to your left (north) for about 2,300 yards (1.3 mile) and to your right (south) for 800 yards (0.4 mile). The Union unit astride the road in front of you and facing you was the Twelfth Pennsylvania Reserves Regiment.

Ellerson's Mill, Beaver Dam Creek, and Old Cold Harbor Road as seen from the Union defensive position. *Battle and Leaders of the Civil War.*

Report of Col. John H. Taggart, USA, Commanding Twelfth Pennsylvania Reserves, Third Brigade, Third Division, Fifth Corps, Army of the Potomac

In anticipation of an attack, rifle pits had been dug on the slope of the hill on both sides of the Cold Harbor road leading from Mechanicsville, which commanded the approaches by the road in that direction. On the afternoon of the 26th it was reported that the enemy were advancing in force, when eight companies of the regiment were at once posted in the rifle pits on both sides of the road, and two companies, B, Captain Mathewson, and C, Captain Gustin, were posted at a rifle pit near Ellison's grist-mill, in advance on the right of the road, which commanded the meadow which lay between our position and the advance of the enemy. Two pieces of artillery of Cooper's battery, under command of First Lieut. James S. Fullerton, were also posted on the brow of the hill in rear of the road over which the enemy were expected to pass. These dispositions made; it was not long before the enemy appeared in large force marching from Mechanicsville. Fire was immediately opened upon them by the two pieces of artillery and by the infantry in the rifle pits, which was returned with great spirit and determination by the advancing force.

The battle raged for an hour with great fury, when I discovered that the enemy were attempting to turn our left flank, two full regiments being deployed along the hill opposite us for that purpose, whose skirmishers had advanced to the creek on the west side of the meadow and were endeavoring to cross some distance to our left. I instantly communicated the fact to Brigadier-General Seymour, who ordered the Seventh Regiment Pennsylvania Reserve Volunteer Corps, Colonel Harvey, a battery of three pieces of artillery, and a Massachusetts regiment into a position on our left, which fortunately prevented the accomplishment of the movement.

The action continued until after dark, lasting some five hours, during which we maintained our ground and kept at bay an overwhelming force of the enemy. The firing at dark closed by mutual consent, the enemy occupying the woods on the hill fronting our position, while the men under my command retained possession of the rifle pits, in which they remained during the night. The loss of the enemy must have been very heavy, as they were in full view of our infantry and artillery at short range while the action lasted and in great force. The cries of their wounded were heard plainly all through the night from our position.[6]

Pender's Brigade was fourth in A. P. Hill's Division's order of march and was committed to the fight at this location. Pender had crossed the Chickahominy River at Meadow Bridge and marched along the road toward Mechanicsville. As he approached Mechanicsville, Pender received orders to deploy into line to the right of Field's Brigade. As he began deploying, he came under artillery fire from the Union troops south of Ellerson's Mill. Pender moved his brigade farther to the right to attack this part of the Federal position. Where you are standing was the center of Pender's right regiment, the Thirty-fourth North Carolina.

Report of Brig. Gen. William D. Pender, CSA, Commanding Pender's Brigade, A. P. Hill's Division, Army of Northern Virginia

Upon reaching Mechanicsville I was ordered by you [A. P. Hill] to support General Field. I at once made my dispositions to do so, but

The defensive position of the Pennsylvania Reserves at Ellerson's Mill. *Battle and Leaders of the Civil War.*

soon found that by taking the direction General Field was going [it] left his right much exposed to a heavy fire of artillery, which was playing at the same time on Pegram's battery with great effect. This artillery was obliquely to the right and lower down Beaver Dam Creek than I saw any troops going. I at once changed the direction of two of my regiments, so as to bring them to the right of this artillery, and succeeded in getting within 150 or 200 yards of it before we were opened upon, but when they did open upon us it was destructive, and the obstacles so great in front, the creek and mill-dam, that after the Thirty-eighth North Carolina had reached these obstacles, and within less than 100 yards of the enemy's rifle pits, they had to fall back. This regiment here advanced boldly and maintained its ground well. The Thirty-fourth North Carolina—the other regiment that had been led by me to the right—had made too much of a detour, and did not come up until the Thirty-eighth had been repulsed. After bringing it up I sent it farther to the right, to make as much diversion as possible in that direction.

General Ripley at this time came up with his brigade, advancing over part of the same ground which had been passed by the Thirty-eighth North Carolina, directly in front of the mill. The Thirty-fourth North Carolina advanced to the creek and there maintained its position until after dark, when I had it withdrawn, so that with this and General Ripley with part of his brigade we held the extreme right of our position until about daylight next morning, when I was relieved. General Ripley had been relieved before.

Other brigades came up during the night. The Twenty-second North Carolina, which had followed to support General Field, when getting to the creek near him, came suddenly upon a regiment of the enemy, just across the run [creek], and after some little parley opened fire, driving the enemy quickly away, but found it impossible to cross. The loss of this regiment here was also very heavy; among others its brave colonel (Conner) received a severe wound in the leg.

I should state, while relating the incidents of this day's fight, that Colonel Hoke (Thirty-eighth North Carolina) was also wounded and had to leave the field. The adjutant of the Thirty-eighth was wounded also, but nobly maintained his position until after dark.[7]

The divisions of Maj. Gens. Daniel H. Hill and James Longstreet were concealed behind the high ground in the vicinity of Stop 2, on the other side of the

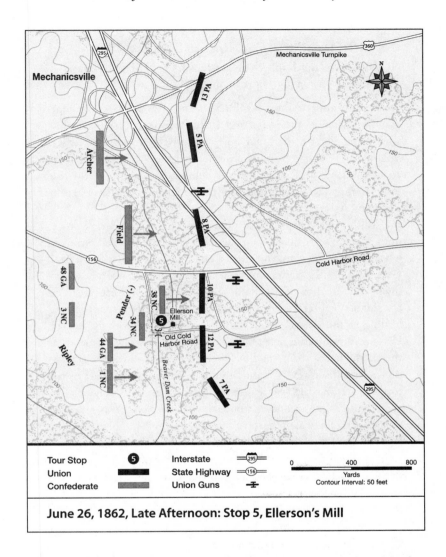

June 26, 1862, Late Afternoon: Stop 5, Ellerson's Mill

Chickahominy River. As A. P. Hill's Division attacked south from Meadow Bridge, it captured the ground east of Mechanicsville Bridge. This was to allow D. H. Hill's and Longstreet's Divisions to cross the Chickahominy. But A. P. Hill secured the ground east of the bridge too late in the afternoon for both divisions to be committed to the fight. D. H. Hill was only able to cross over Ripley's Brigade and send it to support the right of Pender's Brigade.

Two regiments of Ripley's Brigade, the Forty-fourth Georgia and the First North Carolina, attacked across the ground to your right. Both regiments suffered severe casualties.

Report of Brig. Gen. Roswell S. Ripley, CSA, Commanding Ripley's Brigade, D. H. Hill's Division, Army of Northern Virginia

On the morning of Thursday, June 26, the brigade under my command, consisting of the First and Third Regiments North Carolina troops and Forty-fourth and Forty-eighth Regiments of Georgia Volunteers, marched from its position near the Williamsburg road, about 5 miles from Richmond, to a point in the vicinity of the batteries commanding the bridge over the Chickahominy River, on the Mechanicsville turnpike.

With other troops at that point the brigade lay waiting orders until near 4 p.m., when it was ordered to cross the Chickahominy in advance of the division, and effect a junction with the troops of Maj. Gen. A. P. Hill's command, then moving down the Chickahominy in the direction of Mechanicsville. The order was executed and the infantry crossed at once, forming line of battle across the road leading to the village, about half a mile in advance of the bridge. Upon communicating with General A. P. Hill I was informed that the enemy had a strong and well-served battery and force in position near Ellison's Mill, something over a mile to the east of the road, to attack which he had sent Brigadier-General Pender's brigade by the right and other troops to the left, and it was arranged that my brigade was to co-operate. The enemy had opened on the Mechanicsville road and was rapidly verifying the range. My brigade changed front and advanced to the brow of the hill opposite the enemy's battery, expecting, if possible, to use artillery in the attack. While the troops were in motion, I received orders to assault the enemy from General Lee and also from Maj. Gen. D. H. Hill, the latter of whom directed me to send two regiments to support General Pender, on my right, and attack the battery in front with the remainder of my force. The Forty-fourth Georgia, under Col. Robert A. Smith, and the First North Carolina, under Colonel [M. S.] Stokes, marched at once to the right, while the Forty-eighth Georgia, under Colonel [William] Gibson, and Third North Carolina, under Colonel [Gaston] Meares, moved to a position in front of the enemy on their left.

Meanwhile the passage of the Chickahominy by the artillery had been impeded by the broken bridges, and night coming on and it being deemed important to attack the position at once, the advance was ordered along the whole line. General Pender's brigade and the two regiments of my own advanced rapidly on the right, while the remainder of my command moved against the front, driving back the enemy from his advanced positions and closing in upon the batteries and their heavy infantry supports, all of which poured upon our troops a heavy and incessant fire of shell, canister, and musketry. The ground was rugged and intersected by ditches and hedges and covered with abatis a short distance in front of the position to be assaulted. A mill-race, with scarped banks, and in some places waist-deep in water, ran along the front of the enemy at a distance ranging from 50 to 100 yards. To this position our troops succeeded in advancing, notwithstanding the fire of the enemy was exceedingly heavy and our loss extremely severe. Of the Forty-fourth Georgia Col. Robert A. Smith and Lieutenant-Colonel [John B.] Estes fell wounded, the former mortally, besides 2 captains and 10 lieutenants killed and wounded. Of the First North Carolina Colonel Stokes was mortally, Lieutenant-Colonel [John A.] McDowell severely, wounded, and Major [T. L.] Skinner killed, with 6 captains and lieutenants of the regiment killed and wounded, including the adjutant. The Forty-eighth Georgia and Third North Carolina had a more advantageous position, and suffered less severely than the former regiments, although the Third lost its major (Edward Savage), wounded. The loss of non-commissioned officers and privates was heavy in the extreme, amounting in the Forty-fourth Georgia to 321 and in the First North Carolina to 133.

Near dark Capt. A. Burnet Rhett's battery of artillery, attached to my command, succeeded in crossing the broken bridges over the Chickahominy, and was located directly in front of the enemy at about 1,200 yards distance. Captain Rhett opened an effective fire, and soon relieved our infantry from the storm of shell and canister which had been poured upon them. It was soon re-enforced by another battery, and a fire was kept up on the enemy until late in the evening.

Some time after night-fall, under cover of the cannonade, our troops were withdrawn to a point of woods a few hundred yards' distance, near the angle of our line of battle, which position was held by the Third North Carolina and Forty-eighth Georgia and a portion of General Pender's brigade. The fragments of the First North

Carolina and Forty-fourth Georgia were rallied some distance in the rear under some difficulty, owing to the loss of all their field and many of their company officers, who fell while gallantly performing their duty. [8]

A. P. Hill's crossing of the Chickahominy River before Jackson was in position committed his troops to costly and unsuccessful frontal attacks against a strong Union position. From the very start, this choice disrupted Lee's planned turning movement and would cause significant changes in how and where Confederate forces would be situated and deployed for the next several days.

Porter's successful defense at Beaver Dam Creek gave McClellan the opportunity to regain the tactical initiative. A. P Hill's division had been fought to a standstill. Longstreet and D. H. Hill did not get their divisions across the Chickahominy River until after dark and Jackson was still off to the north. McClellan could have sent reinforcement to the north side of the Chickahominy. Part of these reinforcement could protect the Union right flank while the rest joined with the Fifth Corps in an attack on A. P. Hill's, Longstreet's, and D. H. Hill's divisions. McClellan did not reinforce Porter and lost the opportunity to regain the initiative.

Return to your car and drive back to the Old Cold Harbor Road (Highway 156). Turn right onto Old Cold Harbor Road, and drive east for 1.4 mile to Walnut Grove Baptist Church. Turn left into the parking area and park.

Stop 6—Walnut Grove Baptist Church, Lee-Jackson Meeting, Morning of June 27

The small church to the left of the church complex is the original Walnut Grove Baptist Church. On the morning of June 27, Lee and Jackson met here to plan a further attempt for a turning movement. However, this plan was not successful. As a result, a Confederate force would conduct multiple frontal attacks against Porter's Fifth Corps' defensive position at Boatswain's Swamp (Battle of Gaines' Mill) later in the day.

Return to the Old Cold Harbor Road. Turn left and drive 0.1 mile to where Lee-Davis Road (Highway 643) comes from the left and Cold Harbor Road turns to the right. In 1862 this part of the road was called Telegraph Road. Follow Cold Harbor Road to the right and drive for 2.8 miles. Look for the sign "Gaines' Mill Battlefield" where Cold Harbor Road turns to the left, continue straight on to Watt House Road, and drive 0.6 mile to the Watt House parking area. After you have driven 0.3 mile, there will be a fork in the road. Take the road to the left, drive to the parking area, park, and get out of your car.

Stop 7—Battle of Gaines' Mill
(Insufficient Reinforcements for Porter)

The house at the end of the parking lot is the restored Watt House, which was Porter's headquarters. With the house behind you, look back along the road you drove on to the parking area. Boatswain's Swamp (Creek) is about two hundred yards in front of you; when you drove here you crossed it.

You are on the plateau where Porter's Fifth Corps established its defensive position after retreating from Beaver Dam Creek. The northern and western edge of this plateau is traced by the course of Boatswain's Swamp (Creek). The creek begins near the north-south section of Highway 156, which is 2,100 yards (1.2 mile) to your right. From its beginning the creek flows generally southwest for 2,700 yards (1.5 mile), where it turns south and flows for another 2,200 yards (1.3 mile) and joins the Chickahominy River. The high ground just south of the swamp to your right front, in front of you and to your left rear, was the location of the defensive line. You are in the left center of the Union defensive position. The tree line in front of you was not there in 1862. From here the road from New Cold Harbor to Old Cold Harbor and the road that went southwest from Old Cold Harbor were intermittently visible. Boatswain's Swamp and Creek provided a natural obstacle, and Porter set up his defenses behind it.

To defend this position Porter had his three divisions and fourteen batteries (eighty guns). In addition the heavy artillery on the south side of the Chickahominy River was able to fire into the right flank of any Confederate force attacking Porter's left. Brig. Gen. George Sykes's Second Division defended the right of the Fifth Corps line. The division was composed of three brigades; two of them U.S. Regulars. All three of Sykes's brigades were deployed on the battle line. Sykes's right flank was astride the road that came south from Old Cold Harbor. His division's left flank was six hundred yards to your right. Sykes's defensive position was sixteen hundred yards long.

Brig. Gen. George W. Morell's First Division defended the left of the Fifth Corps position. The three brigades of this division were all deployed on the battle line. The right of Morell's division was five hundred yards to your right. From there the line went southwest past your location and continued on for another eleven hundred yards. After the line went five hundred yards

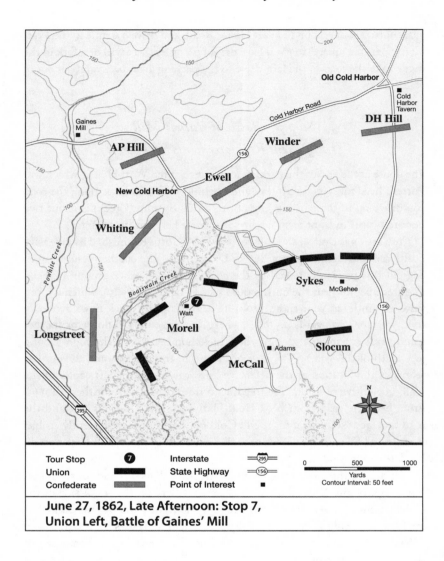

**June 27, 1862, Late Afternoon: Stop 7,
Union Left, Battle of Gaines' Mill**

to your left, it swung back, and went south to its end. Brig. Gen. George A. McCall's Third Division, which had borne the brunt of the fighting at Beaver Dam Creek, was in a reserve position behind Morell.

Confederate forces attacked all along the Union position. Initially, these assaults were piecemeal, but as the afternoon went on, they became coordinated and brought overwhelming force to bear on the defenders.

Report of Maj. Gen. Fitz John Porter, USA, Commanding Fifth Corps, Army of the Potomac

Friday, the 27th of June, after the successful withdrawal of the right wing of the army from Mechanicsville and its encampment on Gaines' and Curtis' farms, near New Bridge, it became necessary for the safety of the material to cover the bridges connecting with the main army across the Chickahominy. For this purpose, the corps was disposed in a semicircle, having its extremities resting on the stream, while the intermediate portion occupied the ground designated by the major-general commanding [McClellan], it being the best possible for defense under the circumstances. Part of the front was covered by the ravine of the [Boatswain's Swamp], covered with trees and underbrush, which partially masked our force and screened the reserves from view.

By this disposition the roads from Cold Harbor and Mechanicsville, which converge at that point, were duly covered and defended. On the front thus formed were posted the divisions of Morell and Sykes, each brigade having in reserve two of its own regiments. Portions of the divisions of artillery of Morell and Sykes were posted to sweep the avenues of approach. The rest were held in reserve. McCall's division formed a second line in rear of the woods skirting the ravine. The troops remained in position waiting the approach of the enemy's columns, known to be advancing in very great force. Believing my force too small to defend successfully this long line, *I asked of General Barnard* [the army's chief engineer], *who had selected and pointed out this position, to represent to the major-general commanding the necessity of re-enforcement* [italics added for emphasis], and he was to send me felling axes for defensive purposes.

About 2 o'clock p.m. the [Confederates] began with their skirmishers to feel for the weakest point of our position, and soon large bodies of infantry, supported by a warm fire of artillery, engaged our whole line. Repulsed in every direction, a few hours of ominous silence ensued, indicating that their troops were being massed for an overwhelming attack. Our infantry and artillery were drawn in toward the center and posted to meet the avalanche. *Re-enforcements were again asked for* [italics added for emphasis].

About 6 o'clock the enemy renewed the attack, advancing immense bodies of infantry, under cover of artillery, along the road from Cold Harbor to Adams' house, immediately upon our right and center, where Sykes' division and Griffin's brigade were placed. This furious attack was successfully resisted and repulsed, but immediately renewed by fresh troops. The reserves were pushed as rapidly as possible into the woods to the support of Griffin, whose regiments were relieved upon the expenditure of their ammunition. This and all our positions were held against the enormous odds, and the enemy were at times driven back by our [regiments] of fresh troops as they were successively thrown into action. At each repulse by us fresh troops were thrown by the enemy upon our exhausted forces, and in such numbers and so rapidly that it appeared as if their reserves were inexhaustible. The action now extending throughout our entire lines, the brigades of McCall were successively thrown forward to give support to Morell's hard-pressed division. The promised re-enforcements (Slocum's division) arrived just as the last of McCall's troops had been sent in to the relief of those of Morell's battalions whose ammunition had been exhausted, or to take the place of those which had been nearly cut to pieces. Newton's brigade, of Slocum's division, being in the advance, was promptly led, regiment after regiment, to the right of Griffin's brigade, of Morell's division, and the left of Sykes' division into the thickest of the fight by its gallant commander, and was soon followed in the same manner by Taylor's brigade, each regiment relieving the regiment in advance as soon as the ammunition of the latter was exhausted.

In the meantime, Sykes, hard pressed on the right, maintaining his ground with all the obstinacy of the regulars and the spirit of the volunteers, required support, and Bartlett's brigade, of Slocum's division, was sent to his relief. A portion, however, of Newton's brigade had already been pushed in to the assistance of his left.

Previous to the arrival of Slocum's brigades, Reynolds, having repulsed the enemy in his front, and hearing the tremendous contest on his left, had, acting under a true maxim and with the generous spirit of a soldier, moved to the sound of cannon, and led his men, regiment after regiment, where our hard-pressed forces required most assistance. As each regiment entered the woods to the relief of their exhausted companions the effect was immediately shown by the enemy being driven before them, as evidenced by the sound of musketry growing more and more distant. Some regiments which had been withdrawn after having exhausted their ammunition reformed, replenished their [ammunition] boxes, and returned, in one case even for the third time, to this unequal contest. For each regiment thrown into action there seemed to be two or three fresh regiments brought up by the enemy, but our men maintained their own, and necessarily repulsed them until the last regiment had been advanced.

As if for a final effort, just as darkness was covering everything from view, the enemy massed his fresh regiments on the right and left and threw them with overpowering force against our thinned and wearied [regiments]. In anticipation of this our artillery, which till now had been well engaged at favorable points of the field in dealing destruction upon the enemy or held in reserve, was now thrown to the front to cover the withdrawal of our retiring troops. The batteries already engaged continued playing on the coming horde, while the others (in all about eighty guns) successively opened as our troops withdrew from in front of their fire, and checked in some places, in others drove back, the advancing masses.

At this juncture the cheering shouts of Brigadier-Generals French's and Meagher's men were heard advancing to our support. Although they came too late to give us the aid required to drive back the already retiring foe, they gave renewed courage and confidence to our men, whose regiments formed under their protection and were all withdrawn that night, with the material and supplies, to the other side of the Chickahominy. Thus, was accomplished the withdrawal of the right wing of the army in execution of the orders of the major-general commanding.[9]

Porter had requested reinforcement. However, only the three brigades of Slocum's division from the Sixth Corps had been sent north across the Chickahominy, although additional forces were available to reinforce Porter.

A. P. Hill's critical decision to commence the attack the previous day had brought the Confederate and Union forces into a stand-up fight at this location. Hill's choice also presented McClellan with an opportunity to defeat Lee's units north of the Chickahominy River. Porter's corps was on dominant terrain that had a natural water barrier in front of it. Lee's attempt to revitalize the turning movement had failed, and his troops were forced into frontal attacks. Sufficient strong reinforcement could have made the defensive position almost prohibitively costly to capture. Some of these reinforcements could have counterattacked Lee's left (east) flank. Success—and there would have been a good chance of it—would have driven Lee back toward the north or northwest and forced him into a defensive position. A decision to strengthen Porter's force could have changed the entire course of events for the Seven Days.

McClellan refused to grasp the opportunity presented to him. He minimally reinforced Porter while large numbers of his troops remained on the south side of the Chickahominy River. Porter's troops were driven off their position, and they crossed the Chickahominy. McClellan then began a series of retreats to the James River.

Return to your car, depart the Watt House parking area, and return to Cold Harbor Road. Turn right on Cold Harbor Road, and drive 1.2 miles to the intersection where the Beulah Church Road comes in from the left and the Cold Harbor Road turns right (south). Shortly after you turn right, you will pass a visitor center and bookstore. You may wish to stop there. Just before the intersection with the Beulah Church Road, turn into the dirt and gravel parking area on the left, and park so you are looking south.

Stop 8—Confederate Left Flank

Units from Ewell's, Winder's and D. H. Hill's Confederate divisions were formed parallel to and on the right (south) side of the road that you drove on. It was from these areas that they attacked the center and right of Porter's position. You are at the extreme left of the Confederate line. This was the left of D. H. Hill's Division. From this location and to your right his brigades moved south and attacked the right of Porter's defensive line. Even though cavalry was stationed on his left flank, the left of D. H. Hill's attacking line was uncovered and exposed. For the next mile the area to your left would have been a good avenue of approach for a Union counterattack against D. H. Hill's Division and Lee's left flank. However, a lack of reinforcements prevented this from happening.

Report of Maj. Gen. Daniel H. Hill, CSA, Commanding D. H. Hill's Division, Army of Northern Virginia

About 9 p.m. [June 26] I received an order from General Lee to co-operate with Major-General Jackson on the Cold Harbor road, going by way of Bethesda Church.

The shorter road, upon which Major-General Jackson marched, being obstructed, he was compelled to turn off and follow in my rear.

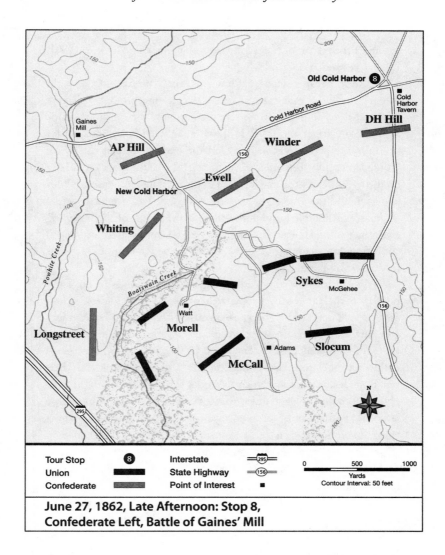

**June 27, 1862, Late Afternoon: Stop 8,
Confederate Left, Battle of Gaines' Mill**

We therefore reached Cold Harbor first, capturing a few wagons, ambulances, and prisoners. The division moved up cautiously to the edge of [Boatswain's] Swamp, where the Yankees were found to be strongly posted, with ten pieces of artillery commanding the only road upon which our guns could be moved. Captain Bondurant's battery was brought into action, but in less than half an hour was withdrawn and badly crippled. By the order of Major-General Jackson the division was moved back to the edge of the woods parallel to the road to cut off the retreat of the enemy from the attack of Major-Generals Longstreet and A. P. Hill.

It soon became apparent, however, that the fire on our right was receding and that the Yankees were gaining ground. Jackson's [Winder's] division and mine were then ordered forward to the support of Longstreet and A. P. Hill, who had been hotly engaged for several hours. My division occupied the extreme left of the whole Confederate line. The order of advance of the division was, Garland on the left, next [G. B.] Anderson, next Rodes, next Colquitt; Ripley being on the extreme right. In advancing we had a dense swamp to cross, with tangled undergrowth, and the radius of the wheeling circle had to be shortened. These combined causes produced much confusion and a lapping of brigades and the separation of regiments from their proper places.

My division now occupied the edge of the wooded swamp, separated from the Yankees by an open field some 400 yards wide. Confederate troops upon our right, subsequently discovered to be Winder's and Lawton's brigades, were advancing across the plain to attack them. I found Generals Anderson and Garland discussing with great enthusiasm the propriety of attacking the Yankees in flank with their two brigades, while Lawton and Winder attacked in front. The only objection to the movement was that a Yankee battery on our extreme left could enfilade our line on its advance. Garland observed, "I don't think it can do much harm, and I am willing to risk it." Anderson responded in the same spirit, and I ordered an advance of the whole division. To prevent the destruction of life [by] the battery I resolved to make an attempt to capture it.

It was now fairly dark, and hearing loud cheers from the Yankees in our immediate front, some 200 yards distant, I ordered our whole advance to halt and wait an expected attack of the enemy. Brigadier-General Winder, occupying the road to Grapevine Bridge, immediately halted, and the whole advance columns were halted also. The cheering, as we afterward learned, was caused by the appearance of the Irish Brigade to cover the retreat. A vigorous attack upon it might have resulted in the total rout of the Yankee army and the capture of thousands of prisoners, but I was unwilling to leave the elevated plateau around McGehee's house to advance in the dark along an unknown road, skirted by dense woods, in the possession of Yankee troops.

The night was spent in caring for the wounded and making preparations for the morning. I drew back the advanced troops several hundred yards to McGehee's house, and sent across the swamp for my division artillery. This, however, did not come up till sunrise next morning. All of the advanced troops of General Jackson reported to me for orders, and with my own were intrusted with guarding the road to Grapevine Bridge. Soon after daylight it was discovered that the Yankees had retreated across the Chickahominy, destroying all the bridges.[10]

The drive from this stop to Stop 9 covers a total of 4.9 miles on three connecting roads. Depart the parking area, and drive south on the Cold Harbor Road (Highway 156), to your right as you drove to the intersection, for 3.2 miles to a bridge crossing the Chickahominy. This is the location of the 1862 Union-constructed Grapevine Bridge. Cross the bridge. When the road goes to four lanes, immediately move to the left lane, and in 0.3 mile turn left onto Old Hanover Road, then in 0.1 mile turn left onto Grapevine Road. Continue driving for 1.3 miles to Meadow Road. After you travel 0.3 mile on Grapevine Road, you will pass the Trent House on your right. If you pause to look, **do not** move off the road—there is a deep ditch there. The Trent House was McClellan's headquarters from June 12 to June 28. At the T-intersection with Meadow Road turn left, drive for one hundred yards, turn into the small parking area to the right of the road, and park. Leave your car and look south across the fields.

Stop 9—Savage Station

Located where the far tree line southeast across the field is today, Savage Station was a stop on the Richmond and York River Railroad and also part of a farm. In addition, a Union field hospital and forward supply dump was located there. To allow the army to retreat, Union forces west of Savage Station fought a rear-guard defense against the forward movement of Magruder's units from the eastern edge of Richmond. Magruder was halted. Jackson was supposed to cross the Chickahominy River and join Magruder, but he did not. During the night, the rear guard marched four miles to the White Oak Bridge.

Return to your car for the drive to Stop 10. Make a U-turn and drive west on Meadow Road for 0.4 mile to the intersection with Dry Bridge Road. You will pass the intersection of Meadow Road and Grapevine Road, and then you will cross over Interstate 295. Turn left (south) on Dry Bridge Road and drive for 1.1 miles to Williamsburg Road (US Highway 60). Turn left into the eastbound lanes, and drive east for 2.6 miles to the intersection with Elko Road (Highway 156). Turn right onto the Elko Road and drive for 3.0 miles to Elko, where you will cross a set of railroad tracks. After you have driven for 2.3 miles from the intersection of US Highway 60 and Elko Road, White Oak Road will intersect from the left. The retreating Union units and the advancing Confederates used both of these roads. After crossing the railroad tracks at Elko, continue on for 0.2 mile, where you will come to a roadside parking area with a marker. This is just before a bridge. Pull off to the right side of the road, near the marker, and get out of your car. Face in the direction you were driving. **Be careful of traffic.**

Stop 10—White Oak Swamp Bridge

Directly in front of you is White Oak Swamp and White Oak Swamp Creek. The swamp extends three and one-half miles to your right (west), with the creek extending even farther. To your left the swamp and creek continue for two miles, then flow into the Chickahominy River. This low, swampy ground was a natural barrier that had to be crossed by the retreating Union army and the Confederate forces in direct pursuit. In 1862 as today, visibility in this area was limited because of the trees and undergrowth.

In 1862 a large body of troops could cross the swamp in a limited number of places. One of the best crossings was where you are now. Another good area was located two miles to your right. Three fords were situated between these two bridged crossing points, and all of the corps of the Army of the Potomac crossed at these locations. Roads from the two crossing sites funneled into the junction at Glendale, where one road then went south over Malvern Hill to the James River. It was at this Glendale choke point that the divisions of Huger, Longstreet, and A. P. Hill were marching to cut off the Union retreat. These Confederate units had bypassed the swamp to the west. Lee was counting on the direct pressure force, now under Jackson, to maintain pressure on the Union rear guard and slow down the retreat.

On the night of June 29, the Union divisions of Brig. Gen. William F. Smith and Brig. Gen. Israel B. Richardson, who had fought a delaying action at Savage Station, marched along the roads you drove over and at dawn crossed the creek in front of you. These two divisions, under the command of Sixth Corps commander Brig. Gen. William B. Franklin, occupied defensive positions on the high ground across the creek from where you are now.

Richardson's division was to the west of the road, and Smith's division was to the east. The last Union unit to cross over destroyed the bridge.

Report of Brig. Gen. Israel B. Richardson, USA, Commanding First Division, Second Corps, Army of the Potomac

Late at night I received an order to act as a rear guard with my division in covering the movement of the army across the White Oak Swamp, and also to take charge personally of the breaking up of the bridge across the creek, so as to make it impracticable for the passage of artillery. My march commenced about 1 o'clock on the 30th of June, and after marching until nearly daybreak in the morning, on coming up to the bridge I found the mass of stragglers from other parts of the army wedged in so as to be unable to move. I impressed them with the necessity of crossing as rapidly as possible or the enemy would be upon us and the rear of the army cut off. By the greatest exertions of myself and staff I succeeded in getting this mass over by sunrise and my own division, and the bridge was broken up and burned by about 10 o'clock a.m. I was now directed by General Sumner to remain here until further orders, the division of General Smith being on my right.[11]

Jackson's Command crossed the Chickahominy River in the early morning hours of June 30. D. H. Hill's Division was the leading unit. Hill marched through Savage Station to the vicinity of White Oak Bridge generally along the same route you drove. Upon arriving on the high ground north of White Oak Swamp, he discovered the bridge had been destroyed, and Union infantry and artillery occupied a defensive position south of the swamp.

Report of Maj. Gen. Daniel H. Hill, CSA, Commanding Hill's Division, Army of Northern Virginia

Jackson's command, my division leading, passed Savage Station early in the morning of the 30th instant, and followed the line of the Yankee retreat toward White Oak Creek. We picked up about 1,000 prisoners and so many arms, that I detached the Fourth and Fifth North Carolina Regiments to take charge of both.

At White Oak Creek we found the bridge destroyed and the Yankee forces drawn up on the other side. Twenty-six guns from my division and five from Whiting's division opened a sudden and unexpected fire upon the Yankee batteries and infantry. A feeble response was attempted, but silenced in a few minutes. Munford's cavalry and my skirmishers crossed over, but the Yankees got some guns under cover of a wood which commanded the bridge, and the cavalry was compelled to turn back. The skirmishers staid over all day and night. We attempted no further crossing that day. [12]

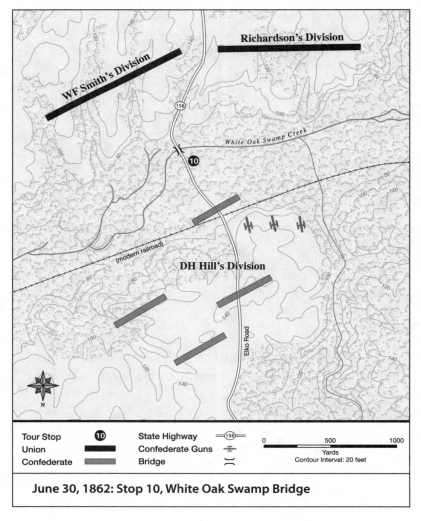

Tour Stop	⑩	State Highway	═156═
Union		Confederate Guns	
Confederate		Bridge	

0   500   1000
Yards
Contour Interval: 20 feet

June 30, 1862: Stop 10, White Oak Swamp Bridge

The artillery that D. H. Hill refers to was located on the higher ground seven hundred yards to your right rear. This artillery was under the command of Jackson's chief of artillery.

Report of Col. Stapleton Crutchfield, CSA, Chief of Artillery, Jackson's Command, Army of Northern Virginia

On Monday, June 30, we crossed the Chickahominy at Grapevine Bridge and moved toward White Oak Swamp, which we reached about 9.30 a.m. At this point the swamp was crossed by a trestle bridge, which the enemy had just fired, while it was commanded by their guns from the opposite hill, and all approach to it prevented by their sharpshooters, who were concealed in a thick wood nearby. After examining the ground, I found it possible with a little work to open a way through the woods to the right of the road on which we advanced, by which our guns could be brought, unseen by the enemy, into position behind the crest of the hill on this side, about 1,000 yards from the enemy's batteries and some 1,200 yards from their infantry. Seven batteries (in all twenty-three guns) were accordingly ordered up from Maj. Gen. D. H. Hill's division. Having met their officers for the first time on that day I do not now readily recall their names, and can only mention the batteries of Capts. T. H. Carter, R. A. Hardaway, G. W. Nelson, A. B. Rhett, James Reilly, and W. L. Balthis (the last two belonging to Brigadier-General Whiting's division) as being of the number.

About 1.45 p.m. we opened suddenly upon the enemy, who had no previous intimation of our position and intention. He only fired four shots in reply and then abandoned the position in extreme haste and confusion. A house nearby (afterward found to have contained subsistence stores) was first either fired by themselves or by our shell and burned down. Captain Wooding's battery was immediately ordered down nearer to the burned bridge to shell out the sharpshooters from the woods, which was soon accomplished, and our cavalry crossed the swamp.

It was then found that the enemy was bringing up a considerable artillery force to take position on the opposite side of the road to his former place and directly opposed to our guns, from which he would be concealed by a thick intervening wood. Capt. G. W. Wooding's battery was therefore withdrawn and our batteries turned in the new direction. The enemy soon opened on us with about eighteen guns, I think, and we replied, though it was extremely difficult to estimate the distance, as the enemy's guns were entirely concealed from view and our only guide was the sound, while our exact position was of course known to him. His fire was rapid and generally accurate, though the nature of the ground afforded us such shelter as to protect us from much loss. The effect of our own fire could not be estimated until we crossed the swamp next day, when there were palpable evidences of its having been much more destructive than that to which we were subjected. This engagement lasted till dusk without intermission. [13]

Report of Brig. Gen. Israel B. Richardson, USA, Continued

Early in the afternoon, while our troops were resting, a heavy cannonade was opened by the enemy on the other side of the creek from a hill partly covered by timber. It appeared to be some three batteries, and they all opened at once. My division stood firmly. The battery of [Capt. George W.] Hazzard's exhausting its ammunition, the captain being wounded and many men and horses disabled, it was replaced by the battery of Captain [Rufus D.] Pettit, which kept up continuous fire until night. After firing away all their ammunition these were now replaced by a battery of Franklin's division, which kept up a fire with two pieces until 12 o'clock at night, when I was ordered again to fall back to form the rear guard. Two of my brigades had been detached during the day [to reinforce at Glendale], and I had only that of [Brig. Gen. William H.] French to cover the movement. The movement was again performed successfully. [14]

Although Col. Thomas Munford and then Brig. Gen. Wade Hampton had found crossing points half a mile or less to your left, Jackson took no action and issued no orders to cross the swamp. Jackson's critical decision to do nothing kept his force idle north of White Oak Swamp. As a result, Confederates did not exert continuous pressure on the Union rear guard, two brigades from Richardson's division reinforced the Union defenders at Glendale. The Confederate divisions were kept from the Glendale battle and Jackson lost the opportunity to flank the defenders at White Oak Bridge, cross the swamp, and position a significant force on the flank and in the rear of the Union defenders at Glendale.

Continue driving south for 1.2 miles to the intersection with the Charles City Road (Highway 156). Turn right, and drive west for 1.1 mile to the intersection of the Willis Church Road, Darbytown Road, and Charles City Road. Turn right, and immediately pull off to the right and stop.

Stop 11—Glendale Intersection

You are at the intersection of the roads that the majority of the Army of the Potomac had to pass through during its retreat to the James River. Lee also had his army pointed toward this intersection in his pursuit and attack to cut off and break up the Union army.

The road in front of you is the Charles City Road. It runs in a northwesterly direction and in two and one-half miles crosses the western end of White Oak Swamp. Lee ordered Huger to march his division down this road and attack the Union forces passing through this intersection.

The road to your left is the Darbytown Road. It has been renamed since 1862. At that time, it did not reach Glendale but intersected the Long Bridge Road about two miles southwest of here. The Long Bridge Road came to this intersection from the southwest. Lee had ordered Longstreet and A. P. Hill to march their divisions around White Oak Swamp, proceed southeast on the Darbytown Road to its intersection with the Long Bridge Road, and then continue northeast on the Long Bridge Road, where they would join Huger in an attack to cut the Army of the Potomac's route of retreat. The road behind you is the Willis Church Road. In 1862 it was also called the Quaker Road, and it was sometimes confused with another road southwest of here with that same name. The Willis Church Road extends south from this intersection for two and three-quarters miles to Malvern Hill, a major defensive position only one mile from the James River. The capture of the Willis Church Road or the Glendale intersection by Confederate forces would have been a disaster for McClellan's army.

McClellan's army was centered on the Glendale Crossroads. The Union commander deployed four corps with a total of nine infantry divisions. The line generally formed an upside-down *L*, which gave the Union force interior lines on the defensive position.

Five hundred yards in front of you was the short part of the *L*, a Union division facing northwest with its left on the Charles City Road. To this division's right were an open space in the defenses and then the two divisions overlooking White Oak Bridge. To the left of the division in front of you, the Union defensive line made a right-angle turn and went south along and west of the Willis Church Road for 1.3 miles. Then there was another gap

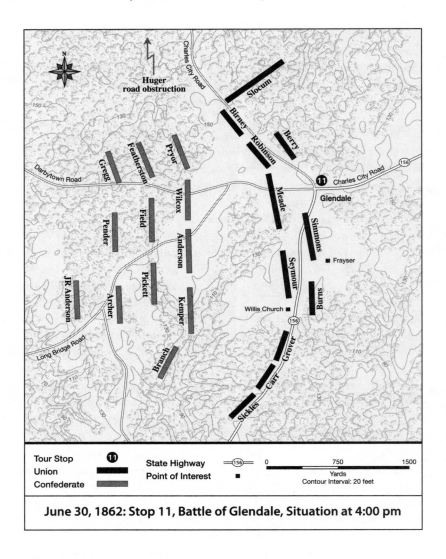

June 30, 1862: Stop 11, Battle of Glendale, Situation at 4:00 pm

for about one mile, with the left of the position being occupied by troops on Malvern Hill.

Lee had envisioned a large coordinated attack against the entire Union position on June 30. Jackson's Command was supposed to cross White Oak Swamp at the bridge, drive off the defenders, and then be in a position to outflank the right of the Union defenses. Huger's Division was supposed to attack the Union troops in front of you. Concurrently, Longstreet and A. P. Hill would strike the position at the crossroads and along the Willis Church

Road. Jackson did not cross White Oak Swamp, and Huger was held up by the obstructions on the Charles City Road. This left only Longstreet and A. P. Hill to carry the fight, and they were unsuccessful. At the end of the day Union forces controlled the crossroads and Willis Church Road, and during the night they successfully retreated to Malvern Hill.

Report of Gen. Robert E. Lee, CSA, Commanding Army of Northern Virginia

Jackson reached Savage Station early on the 30th. He was directed to pursue the enemy on the road he had taken and Magruder to follow Longstreet by the Darbytown road. As Jackson advanced, he captured such numbers of prisoners and collected so many arms that two regiments had to be detached for their security. His progress was arrested at White Oak Swamp. The enemy occupied the opposite side and obstinately resisted the reconstruction of the bridge.

Longstreet and A. P. Hill, continuing their advance on the 30th, soon came upon the enemy strongly posted across the Long Bridge road, about 1 mile from its intersection with the Charles City road. Huger's route led to the right of this position, Jackson's to the rear, and the arrival of their commands was awaited to begin the attack.

On the 29th General Holmes had crossed from the south side of James River with part of his division.

On the 30th, re-enforced by General Wise with a detachment of his brigade, he moved down the river road and came upon the line of the retreating army near Malvern Hill. Perceiving indications of confusion, General Holmes was ordered to open upon the column with artillery. He soon discovered that a number of batteries, advantageously posted, supported by an infantry force superior to his own and assisted by the fire of the gunboats in the James River, guarded this part of the line.

Magruder, who had reached the Darbytown road, was ordered to re-enforce Holmes, but being at a greater distance than had been supposed, he did not reach the position of the latter in time for an attack.

Huger reported that his progress was obstructed, but about 4 p.m. firing was heard in the direction of the Charles City road, which was supposed to indicate his approach. Longstreet immediately opened with one of his batteries to give notice of his presence. This brought on the engagement, but Huger not coming up, and Jackson having been unable to force the passage of White Oak Swamp, Longstreet and [A. P.] Hill were without the expected support. The superiority of numbers and advantage of position were on the side of the enemy.

The battle raged furiously until 9 p.m. By that time the enemy had been driven with great slaughter from every position but one, which he maintained until he was enabled to withdraw under cover of darkness.

At the close of the struggle nearly the entire field remained in our possession, covered with the enemy's dead and wounded. Many prisoners, including a general of division, were captured, and several batteries, with some thousands of small-arms, taken. Could the other commands have co-operated in the action the result would have proved most disastrous to the enemy.

After the engagement Magruder was recalled to relieve the troops of Longstreet and Hill. His men, much fatigued by their long, hot march, arrived during the night.[15]

Maj. Gen. James Longstreet was the tactical commander on the field and had control of his division and A. P. Hill's division.

Report of Maj. Gen. James Longstreet, CSA, Commanding Longstreet's Division, Army of Northern Virginia

Our forces came upon the enemy at Frazier's farm about noon, when the enemy's skirmishers were reported as advancing. Colonel Jenkins, commanding the Second Brigade, was directed to ascertain the condition of the enemy. After driving in his pickets it was found that he was in force and position, ready for battle. My own division was put in position for attack or defense at once, and one of Maj. Gen. A. P. Hill's brigades (Branch's) ordered forward to support my right flank, the rest of Hill's division being left for the time on the road to secure the right or to move up to support the front.

About this time information was received that Major-General Magruder was in rear in easy supporting distance; but as information was also received that the enemy was in force in front of Major-General Holmes, it was deemed advisable to order Magruder's forces to join Holmes, about 3 miles off to our right.

After getting into position artillery fire was opened about 3 p.m. upon the enemy, apparently from the Charles City road. Taking this for Huger's attack, and thinking that his troops (rather fresh) would expect early co-operation, I ordered several batteries forward hurriedly in order to assure those troops that we were in position. The enemy's batteries returned the fire immediately and with great rapidity. One battery was found to be so near our front line that I ordered Colonel Jenkins to silence it. The enemy was found to be in such force there, however, that the engagement was brought on at once (4 o'clock). Troops were thrown forward as rapidly as possible to the support of the attacking columns. Owing to the nature of the ground that concert of action so essential to complete success could not obtain, particularly attacking such odds against us and in position. The enemy, however, was driven back slowly and steadily, contesting the ground inch by inch. He succeeded in getting some of his batteries off the field, and, by holding his last position until dark, in withdrawing his forces under cover of night.[16]

If you wish to visit the area where Huger's Division was halted by the road obstacles, follow these instructions. If not, turn around and follow the instructions for the drive to Stop 13.

Continue driving on the Charles City Road for two miles to the intersection of Banstead Road on your left. Turn left onto Banstead Road, do a U-turn when convenient, and drive back to Charles City Road. Just before Charles City Road, pull to the side of the road and stop. Respect private property.

Stop 12—Obstacles

Huger's Division bivouacked the night of June 29–30 about one mile to your left. In the morning the soldiers marched toward you on the Charles City Road, and when they reached this vicinity they found the road, which in 1862 had woods on both sides, obstructed with felled trees. Rather than clear the trees away, Huger decided to cut a new parallel road. This proved a useless exercise, as Union troops were able to continue obstructing the road as fast as the Confederates cut the new route.

As you drive back to the Glendale Crossroads, in 0.5 mile you will come to an area that will provide you a good representation of the vegetation as it appeared in 1862.

If you did not drive to Stop 11, turn around so you are facing south, and follow the instructions below beginning with the second sentence.

Turn right onto the Charles City Road and drive 2.0 miles back to the Willis Church Road, Darbytown Road, and Charles City Road intersection. Continue straight through the intersection onto the Willis Church Road. Drive south on Willis Church Road for 2.2 miles to the Carter's Mill Road on your right. As you drive along the Willis Church Road to just beyond the church, you will be passing behind or along the Union defensive positon. Turn right on the Carter's Mill Road, and drive 0.5 mile to where a dirt road intersects from the left. This point is just past a small wood. Turn around here and drive back 0.3 mile to the pedestrian crossing. Park on the side of the road, as far off the road as you can. **Be careful of traffic.** Leave your car and walk to your right, as you were driving, for 175 yards to the artillery in the open field. At the guns, face left and look in the direction they are pointed; toward the Union defensive position on Malvern Hill.

Stop 13—Malvern Hill

Position A, Confederate Right

You are in the right of the Confederate position on July 1. The left of Lee's position is where D. H. Hill's Division deployed astride and to the left (east)

Willis Methodist Church. *Battle and Leaders of the Civil War.*

of the Willis Church Road, which you drove on. You will go to the left later. Before the day was over, ten brigades were deployed where you are and forward.

One thousand yards directly in front of you was the center of the Union position. The position extended to your right to the Crew House, which you can't see from here today because of the trees. From the center the Federals' location went left to the West House (the white house 1,100 yards in front of you), past this house for a distance, then curved around to the southeast and south to conform to the contour of the hill. Infantry and artillery occupied this position.

Report of Gen. Robert E. Lee, CSA, Commanding Army of Northern Virginia

Jackson formed his line with Whiting's division on his left and D. H. Hill's on his right, one of Ewell's brigades occupying the interval. The rest of Ewell's and Jackson's [Winder's] own divisions were held in reserve. Magruder was directed to take position on Jackson's right, but before his arrival two of Huger's brigades came up and were placed next to [D. H.] Hill. Magruder subsequently formed on the right of these brigades, which, with a third of Huger's, were placed under his command. Longstreet and A. P. Hill were held in reserve and took no part in the engagement. Owing to ignorance of the country, the dense forests impeding necessary communication, and the extreme difficulty of the ground, the whole line was not formed until a late hour in the afternoon. The obstacles presented by the woods and swamp made it impracticable to bring up a sufficient amount of artillery to oppose successfully the extraordinary force of that arm employed by the enemy, while the field itself afforded us few positions favorable for its use and none for its proper concentration. Orders were issued for a general advance at a given signal, but the causes referred to prevented a proper concert of action among the troops. D.H. Hill pressed forward across the open field and engaged the enemy gallantly, breaking and driving back his first line; but a simultaneous advance of the other troops not taking place, he found himself unable to maintain the ground he had gained against the overwhelming numbers and numerous batteries of the enemy. Jackson sent to his support his own division and that part of Ewell's which was in reserve, but owing to the increasing darkness and intricacy of the forest and swamp they did not arrive in time to render the desired assistance. Hill was therefore compelled to abandon part of the ground he had gained after suffering severe loss and inflicting heavy damage upon the enemy. On the right the attack was gallantly made by Huger's and Magruder's commands. Two brigades of the former commenced the action; the other two were subsequently sent to the support of Magruder and Hill. Several determined efforts were made to storm the hill at Crew's house. The brigades advanced bravely across the open field, raked by the fire of a hundred cannon and the musketry of large bodies of infantry. Some were broken and gave way, others approached close to the guns, driving back the infantry, compelling the advanced batteries to retire to escape capture, and mingling their dead with those of the enemy. For want of concert among the attacking columns their assaults were too weak to break the Federal line, and after struggling gallantly, sustaining and inflicting great loss, they were compelled successively to retire. Night was approaching when the attack began, and it soon became difficult to distinguish friend from foe. The firing continued until after 9 p.m., but no decided result was gained. Part of the troops were withdrawn to their original positions, others remained on the open field, and some rested within a hundred yards of the batteries that had been so bravely but vainly assailed. [17]

Lee's concept for July 1 was that two "grand batteries" would be situated to place heavy preparatory artillery fire on the Union position, followed by an infantry attack. The "right grand battery" was to be located in your vicinity and would contain approximately fifty guns. The "left grand battery" was to be in position to the left of the Willis Church Road, where it was believed at least fifty and maybe up to one hundred guns could be used. In actual practice, this concept did not materialize. Poor artillery organization and confusion on the roads leading to Malvern Hill greatly reduced the number of guns in these two locations—on the right, four batteries with twenty guns, and on the left, five batteries with a maximum of twenty guns. The Union artillery was able to neutralize this artillery, and the guns were withdrawn.

With the failure of the artillery plan, Lee had ridden to a position to your left rear to determine whether there was an avenue of approach to flank the defenses on their right. It was here, out of sight of the Malvern Hill positions, that he received a report that Armistead's Brigade was moving forward in an attack and Union batteries were withdrawing. Without verifying this information, Lee ordered Magruder to attack. This directive committed the Confederate infantry on the right and D. H. Hill's Division on the left into a frontal attack.

Report of Capt. Carey F. Grimes, CSA, Commanding Portsmouth (Va.) Battery, Huger's Division Army of Northern Virginia

On that day I was on the Charles City road with [Brig. Gen. William] Mahone's brigade, and was ordered back to Darbytown road to report to [Brig. Gen. Lewis A.] Armistead, which I immediately did. When I arrived at the position and reported General Armistead told me that a captain had just reported his battery to him for duty, and directed me report to the first general I saw, and [Brig. Gen. Ambrose R.] Wright being the first, I reported to him, and while talking with General Wright General Armistead's aide came up, stating that General Armistead had become disgusted with the captain that had reported his battery to him and had driven him with his battery from the field, and that he wished to see General Wright. General Wright asked me to ride with him, which I did. When we found General Armistead he told General Wright that the captain alluded to above had formed so many excuses about getting his battery on the field that he had driven him from the field, and that he wanted General Wright to send a battery that was willing to go in and engage the enemy. General Wright told him he had one, naming mine. General Armistead asked me if I could carry my battery on the hill. I told him if any battery in the world could go mine could. He directed General Wright to show me the position to take, which he did. I found the enemy with their batteries planted and their infantry drawn up in line of battle at about 1,200 yards distant. I then went to the rear for my battery and carried it on the field. As soon as the battery entered the field the enemy opened fire on it, killing 1 man and wounding 3 and killing 1 horse and wounding 2 before I fired a gun. I unlimbered and commenced firing as soon as possible and with telling effect on the enemy.

I remained on the field about two hours. Lost 3 men killed outright and 8 wounded; 2 of them have since died. I lost 10 horses killed and 7 wounded; 1 of them has since died. My horse was killed, also my first lieutenant's horse. I had so many horses killed and wounded that it took three trips to get my guns all off.[18]

Late in the afternoon the Confederate infantry in this area made a series of unsuccessful and costly attacks against the Union position. Magruder provides an overview of the attack from this location.

Report of Maj. Gen. John B. Magruder, CSA, Commanding Magruder's Command, Army of Northern Virginia

General Lee then directed me to place my troops on the right of Huger's, who in the mean time had formed on the right of Jackson. This I did as far as the ground would permit, placing my three divisions *en échelon* to the right and rear.

The enemy having reached these heights and placed himself in communication with his gunboats on the river, I was satisfied from the position of his lines, and from the cheering which had taken place when his troops were thus reassembled, that the whole army of McClellan was in our front. His batteries of artillery were numerous and were collected into two large bodies, strongly supported by infantry, and commanded perfectly the meadow on our right and the field in our front, except the open ravines formed by the undulations of the ground.

I then received an order from General Lee, through Captain Dickinson, assistant adjutant-general, to advance rapidly, press forward my whole line as the enemy were reported to be getting off; General Armistead having repulsed, driven back, and followed up a heavy body of the enemy's skirmishers.

I gave the order that Wright's brigade, supported by Mahone's, should advance and attack the enemy's batteries on the right; that Jones' division, expected momentarily, should advance on the front, and Ransom's brigade should attack on the left; my plan being to hurl about 15,000 men against the enemy's batteries and supporting infantry; to follow up any successes they might obtain, and, if unable to drive the enemy from his strong position, to continue the fight in front by pouring in fresh troops; and in case they were repulsed to hold strongly the line of battle where I stood, to prevent serious disaster to our own arms.

The fire of musketry and artillery now raged with terrific fury. The battlefield was enveloped in smoke, relieved only by flashes from the lines of the contending troops. Round shot and grape crashed through the woods, and shells of enormous size, which reached far beyond the headquarters of our gallant commander-in-chief, burst amid the artillery parked in the rear. Belgian missives and Minie balls lent their aid to this scene of surpassing grandeur and sublimity. Amid all our gallant troops in front pressed on to victory, now cheered by the rapid fire of friends on their left, as they had been encouraged in their advance by the gallant brigades on the right, commanded by Generals Wright and Mahone. Nevertheless, the enemy from his strong position and great numbers, resisted stoutly

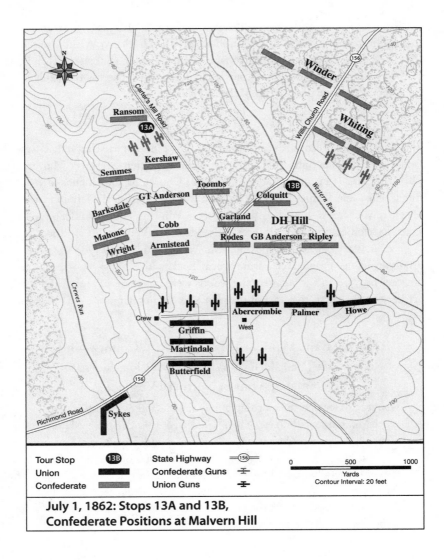

July 1, 1862: Stops 13A and 13B,
Confederate Positions at Malvern Hill

the onset of our heroic bands, and bringing into action his heavy reserves, some of our men were compelled to fall back. They were easily rallied, however, and led again with fury to the attack.

Darkness had now set in and I thought of withdrawing the troops, but, as we had gained many advantages, I concluded to let the battle subside and to occupy the field, which was done to within 100 yards of the enemy's guns.[19]

Return to your car. Continue driving on Carter's Mill Road for 0.2 mile to the intersection with Willis Church Road. Turn left onto Willis Church Road and drive 0.1 mile to the parsonage parking area on your right. Turn in to the parking area, park, leave your car, and look south across the fields to the Union defensive position on Malvern Hill.

Position B, Confederate Left

The West House is 650 yards in front of you. The center of the Union defenses is 750 yards to your right front, just east of the road that goes over Malvern Hill. This road is a continuation of the Willis Church Road, which is to your right. Maj. Gen. Daniel H. Hill's division was deployed to the left and right of where you are. Behind this division were Whiting's and Winder's Divisions. Jackson commanded all forces this side of the Willis Church Road.

The artillery plan was to position the "left grand battery" 700 yards behind you in the Poindexter Farm's wheat field, with a range to the Union position of 1,300 to 1,500 yards. The woods were not there in 1862. Like the artillery on the right, this part of the plan also did not happen.

Report of Capt. William T. Poague, CSA, Commanding Rockbridge (Va.) Battery, Winder's Division, Jackson's Command, Army of Northern Virginia

About 10 o'clock on the morning of July 1, while following the brigade on the march near Frazier's farm, I received an order from Major-General Jackson to hurry on to the front and report to Major-General Whiting. Not being able to find the latter officer, by direction of General Jackson I took position in a wheat field on the left of Balthis' battery (Staunton Artillery), which had just preceded us. My guns were posted behind the crest of a ridge, by which they were to some extent protected from the enemy's fire.

Shortly after opening fire the impression got out by some means that all the batteries were ordered to leave the field. Not being able to trace it to an authoritative source, I ordered my pieces to continue firing. One or two batteries in the mean time left the field. Captain Balthis soon exhausted his ammunition, and shortly afterward left the field. By this time Lieutenant Carpenter had gotten two pieces in position and opened fire.

The fire of the enemy's batteries was most terrific, and in the main very accurate. That the loss on our side was not much heavier is owing to the protection afforded by our position.

The detachment of the 6-pounder was now so much reduced as not to be able to work the gun; it was sent off the field, and the remainder of the detachment distributed among the other pieces. Finding that the contest was a very unequal one, having the fire of several batteries concentrated upon five guns on our side, my pieces were ordered to cease firing. The gun of Lieutenant Carpenter, next to us, also ceased at my suggestion. My object was to induce the enemy to hold up until we could get other batteries to our assistance. Two more batteries were then brought into position. Our guns again opened, under direction of Major Whiting, but elicited only a feeble response from the enemy. After a few rounds our batteries ceased firing. About 5 o'clock I obtained permission to go to the rear for ammunition.

The following are the casualties which occurred during this artillery engagement: Killed— privates, 2. Wounded— non-commissioned officers, 1; privates, 9. One horse was killed and several disabled.[20]

D. H. Hill's report gives a good over view of the fighting on the Confederate left.

Report of Maj. Gen. Daniel H. Hill, CSA, Commanding Hill's Division, Jackson's Command, Army of Northern Virginia

By the order of Major-General Jackson the division was halted in the woods and an examination made of the ground. The Yankees were found to be strongly posted on a commanding hill, all the approaches to which could be swept by his artillery, and were guarded by swarms of infantry securely sheltered by fences, ditches, and ravines. Tier after tier of batteries were grimly visible on the plateau, rising in the form of an amphitheater. One flank was protected by Turkey Creek and the other by gunboats. We could only reach the first line of batteries by traversing an open space of from 300 to 400 yards, exposed to a murderous fire of grape and canister from the artillery and musketry from the infantry. If that first line was carried, another and another still more difficult remained in the rear. I had expressed my disapprobation of a farther pursuit of the Yankees to the commanding general and to Major-Generals Jackson and Longstreet even before I knew of the strength of their position. An examination now satisfied me that an attack could not but be hazardous to our arms.

About 2 o'clock, I think, I received a note from General Jackson, inclosing one from Col. R. H. Chilton: chief of General Lee's staff, saying that positions were selected from which our artillery could silence the Yankee artillery, and as soon as that was done Brigadier-General Armistead would advance with a shout and carry the battery immediately in his front. This shout was to be the signal for a general advance, and all the troops were then to rush forward with fixed bayonets. I sent for all my brigade commanders and showed them the note. Instead of ordering up 100 or 200 pieces of artillery to play on the Yankees, a single battery (Moorman's) was ordered up and knocked to pieces in a few minutes. One or two others shared the same fate of being beat in detail. Not knowing how to act under these circumstances, I wrote to General Jackson that the firing from our batteries was of the most farcical character. He repeated the order for a general advance at the signal of the shouting from General Armistead.

While conversing with my brigade commanders shouting was heard on our right, followed by the roar of musketry. We all agreed that this was the signal agreed upon, and I ordered my division to advance. This, as near as I could judge, was about an hour and a half before sundown. The division fought heroically and well, but fought in vain. [Brig. Gen. Samuel] Garland, in my immediate front, showed all his wonted courage and enthusiasm, but he needed and asked for re-enforcements. I sent Lieutenant-Colonel [J. M.] Newton, Sixth Georgia, to his support, and observing a brigade by a fence in our rear, I galloped back to it and found it to be that of

Brigadier-General [Robert] Toombs. I ordered it forward to support Garland and accompanied it. The brigade advanced handsomely to the brow of the hill, but soon retreated in disorder. [Col. John B.] Gordon, commanding Rodes' brigade, pushed gallantly forward and gained considerable ground, but was forced back. The gallant and accomplished [Col. Gaston] Meares, Third North Carolina Regiment, Ripley's brigade, had fallen at the head of his regiment, and that brigade was streaming to the rear. [Col. Alfred H.] Colquitt's and Brig. Gen. George B.] Anderson's brigades had also fallen back. [Brig. Gen. Robert] Ransom's brigade had come up to my support from Major-General Huger. A portion of it came, but without its Brigadier- It moved too far to the left and became mixed up with the mass of troops near the parsonage on the Quaker road, suffering heavily and effecting little. Brigadier-General Winder was sent up by Major-General Jackson, but he came too late, and also went to the same belt of woods near the parsonage, already over-crowded with troops. Finally, Major-General [Richard S.] Ewell came up, but it was after dark and nothing could be accomplished. I advised him to hold the ground he had gained and not to attempt a forward movement.

The battle of Malvern Hill might have been a complete and glorious success had not our artillery and infantry been fought in detail. My division batteries, having been three times engaged, had exhausted all their ammunition and had been sent back for a fresh supply. Again, the want of concert with the infantry divisions was most painful. [21]

Lee's critical decision to attack extended the combat between the two adversaries for another day. Had he not ordered the attack, there would not have been a major action at Malvern Hill on July 1. During the night the Army of the Potomac probably would have retreated to an enclave on the James River.

Return to your car for the drive to Stop 13, Position C. Drive from the parking area, turn left onto Willis Church Road, and drive 0.4 mile to the park road to your right. Turn right and drive to the parking area, park, leave your car, and look south across the fields to the Confederate positions.

Stop 13, Position C—The Union Defense

You are standing in the center of the Union defensive position, and as you face north you are looking at the line of Confederate infantry that attacked here. Five hundred yards in front of you is the intersection of the Willis Church and Carter's Mill Roads, which marks the center of the attacking force. The right Confederate artillery position was situated 1,000 yards to your left front. Infantry occupied and attacked from positions forward of this artillery. The left Confederate artillery position was 1,300 yards to your right front. The woods were not there. D. H. Hill's Division was deployed 650 yards to your right front.

The Crew House is to your left, and the West House is to your right. Brig. Gen. George W. Morell's First Division, Fifth Corps was positioned from the Crew House to the road on your right. Morell had deployed his three brigades one behind the other: Griffin's, Martindale's, then Butterfield's. This provided him a defense in depth. Sykes's division was deployed to Morell's left rear, facing west and protecting the left flank. Brig. Gen. Darius N. Couch's First Division, Fourth Corps was positioned across the road. All three of Couch's brigades were deployed on the battle line. Echeloned to Couch's right rear were the Second and Third Corps, which faced east to protect the right flank and provide reinforcements if necessary. The army artillery reserve was located to the rear of the defensive position.

Crew House. *Battle and Leaders of the Civil War.*

Report of Brig. Gen. Fitz John Porter, USA,
Commanding Fifth Corps, Army of the Potomac

The position in which we were thrown had certain elements of great strength, and was the best adapted for a battlefield of any with which we have so far been favored. An elevated plateau covered the converging roads and was fronted to a certain extent with defensible ravines and low grounds, over which our artillery had excellent play. The division of General Morell was placed on the right of the line, with a portion of his division artillery and of Hunt's reserve artillery; the division of General Sykes on the left, with the same support, and the reserve artillery, under Colonel Hunt, advantageously posted for general efficiency, crowning the crest of Malvern Hill. In this position the corps lay on its arms during the night and waited the attack, which took place at about 4 in the afternoon of the 1st of July.

Couch's division . . . remained in support of our immediate right, and, like our own force, lay on its arms through the intermediate time.

On the following morning, July 1, the lines were visited and rectified by the major-general commanding, and Generals Heintzelman and Sumner, who had retired from White Oak Swamp within our

West House, Crew House in the distance. *Battle and Leaders of the Civil War.*

lines during the night, took position on the right of Couch, prepared to resist attack or give support to the left and center, as circumstances should require. Our position was strengthened by the arrival of heavy artillery under Colonel Tyler, whose ten siege guns were posted so as to control the River road and sweep our left flank, and by firing over the heads of our own men to reach the enemy.

At about 1 o'clock p.m. the enemy commenced with his artillery and skirmishers, feeling along our whole front, and kept up a desultory firing till about 4 with but little effect.

The same ominous silence which had preceded the attack in force at Gaines' Mill now intervened, lasting till about 6 o'clock, at which time the enemy opened upon as suddenly with the full force of his artillery, and at once began to push forward his columns of infantry to the attack of our positions. Regiment after regiment, and sometimes whole brigades, were thrown against our batteries, but our infantry withheld their fire till they were within short distance (artillery mowing them down with canister), dispersed the columns in every case, and in some instances followed the retiring mass, driving them with the bayonet, capturing prisoners, and also flags and other trophies.

This contest was maintained by Morell's and Couch's divisions, the former supported by Sykes, who had thrown some of his regiments to the front and dispersed a large column attempting to take us in flank. A portion of the reserve artillery was also here in action. While the battle was proceeding, seeing that the enemy was pressing our men and accumulating his masses to pour fresh troops upon them, I called for aid from General Sumner, which call was promptly responded to by the arrival of General Meagher, with his brigade, followed by that of Sickles, which General Heintzelman voluntarily and generously sent to complete the contest. These brigades I posted—Sickles on the right of Couch and Meagher on the left of Morell and in their support—with instructions to push their regiments forward in echelon of about 100 paces, extending to the rear from the right or left of Couch's division, to relieve those in advance whose ammunition had been expended and to drive the enemy. These directions were promptly and successfully executed. McCall's (now Seymour's) division was held in reserve.

In the meantime, Colonel Hunt hastened and brought up artil-

> lery to relieve the batteries whose ammunition had been exhausted and who had successfully borne the brunt of the engagement throughout the day. The lateness of the hour (9 p.m.) did not permit us to pursue the enemy farther, maintaining due regard to the security of the army, of which we were simply a rear guard, even had we had ammunition and provisions, in both of which particulars our men were sadly deficient.[22]

To the left and right from where you stand was a line of Union artillery. Six artillery batteries were stationed along the line of the infantry facing north. During the fighting, nine batteries from the army artillery reserve reinforced this position.

To your right and across the road was the position of Battery A, Fifth U.S. Artillery, commanded by Lieut. Adelbert Ames. This battery was armed with six 12-pound Napoleons smoothbore cannon. Firing solid shot this gun had an effective range of approximately 1,500 yards. At ranges less than four hundred yards, with a 4.6 inch bore diameter and firing canister it was devastating. During the fighting Ames's battery fired 1,392 rounds of ammunition. Each cannon would have had four ammunition chests, each chest capable of

Union Artillery and Infantry on Malvern Hill. *Battle and Leaders of the Civil War.*

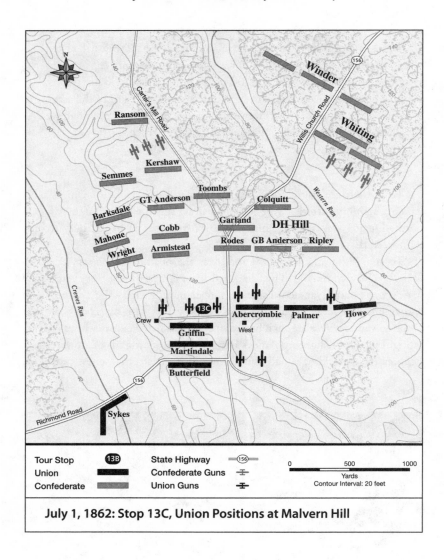

July 1, 1862: Stop 13C, Union Positions at Malvern Hill

holding 32 rounds of ammunition. This would provide 128 rounds per cannon, or 768 rounds for all six cannons. During the fighting Ames had to bring up a minimum of 624 additional rounds, and he probable brought up more. To accomplish this his caisson and limbers must have been in constant motion back to the ammunition trains and then returning to the firing position.

Report of Lieut. Adelbert Ames, USA,
Commanding Battery A, Fifth U.S. Artillery,
Second Brigade, Artillery Reserve, Army of the Potomac.

The battery was in position in a field at distances varying from 400 to 1,100 yards from woods occupied by the enemy. In the forenoon a heavy cannonading was opened upon us and continued at intervals during the day. Early in the afternoon the enemy charged a battery on our right, but were entirely cut up, with loss of their colors. In this instance our canister was very effective. Vigorous attempts were afterward made by heavy masses to turn our left. A heavy artillery fire was poured into them, canister being used from time to time. After night-fall all our ammunition but a few rounds of canister were expended. To use them to advantage we maintained our position for some time under a heavy musketry fire. During the battle 1,392 rounds of ammunition were expended. To obtain this quantity the caissons were sent to the rear as soon as emptied.

During the time we were in position two or three batteries were successively in position on our left and three or four on our right, being relieved as their ammunition was expended.[23]

Brig. Gen. George W. Morell's First Division Fifth Corps defended the ground from the road to your right to the area of the Crew House to your left. Morell positioned all three of his brigades in three successive separate lines, one behind the other. From front to rear they were the brigades of: Brig. Gen. Charles Griffin, Brig. Gen. John H. Martindale, and Brig. Gen. Daniel Butterfield. All of the artillery along this part of the position was placed under Griffin command. He was a pre-war experienced artillery officer and ensure the combined fire of the batteries were used to great effect.

Report of Brig. Gen. Charles Griffin, USA,
Commanding Second Brigade, First Division,
Fifth Corps, Army of the Potomac

General Porter placed the artillery under my command. It was supported on the right by Couch's division. Not far from 10 o'clock the enemy advanced two brigades in front of Couch's right, approaching so close as to throw their musket balls into our batteries, but by a quick concentration of the fire of the four batteries on the field they were soon repulsed. About two hours afterward the enemy attempted an advance upon our extreme left with what appeared to be two brigades, forming in the open field, but the same artillery fire caused him to break and retreat in the greatest disorder. An hour, perhaps, after this the enemy attempted the same maneuver near our right and along the road by which the troops came up, but was again handsomely repulsed by our artillery fire, leaving a stand of colors on the field, which fell into our hands. Here Couch's right wing advanced and drove the enemy far through the wood.

After this a sharp fire was kept up by skirmishers and artillery until 5.30 o'clock, when the enemy made his final and fiercest attack on our left. The artillery continued its effective fire until the enemy arrived within a few yards of our batteries, when the supporting regiments gallantly moved forward and repulsed him.

The casualties were as follows: Killed, 79; wounded, 414; missing, 38; an aggregate of 531.[24]

Throughout the fighting regiments from Martindale's and Butterfield's brigades were sent forward to reinforce Griffin.

Malvern Hill was a clear Union victory. That night again refusing to use the advantage gained McClellan ordered his army to continue its retreat to Harrison's Landing / Berkeley Plantation on the James River.

If you wish, you may end your tour here and return to Richmond or the various interstates. If you want to follow the retreat to Harrison's Landing/ Berkeley Plantation, use the next set of driving instructions.

Drive back to the Willis Church Road. Turn right and drive on the Willis Church Road for 1.1 mile to the New Market Road. Turn left onto the new Market Road (Highway 5) ,and drive east for 8.1 miles to the Herring Creek Road, which is just before a bridge. Turn right onto Herring Creek Road (sign for Berkeley Plantation). Follow the road to the right for 0.2 mile to Harrison's Landing Road on the right. Drive between the two brick columns and on Harrison's Landing Road for 0.6 mile, then turn right into the parking area.

Stop 14—Berkeley Plantation/Harrison's Landing

You are at Berkeley Plantation / Harrison's Landing. The brick plantation house was built in 1726. When the Army of the Potomac retreated to this location, it occupied a defensive position four miles wide and two miles deep, with the flanks anchored on two creeks and the forward line on Evelington Heights. The James River flowed along the rear of the position and could be used to bring supplies, ammunition, and reinforcements. Gunboats could also reinforce the army's artillery.

In early July Abraham Lincoln visited McClellan and the army. Although the president and the army commander discussed matters, they made no decisions. On July 25 Maj. Gen. Henry W. Halleck, newly appointed general-in-chief, visited McClellan. Their conversation centered around what McClellan's next move would be. When Halleck returned to Washington, he thought he and McClellan had decided on a future course of action. However, McClellan sent a message saying he would require considerable reinforcement before he could move. Halleck responded by ordering the Army of the Potomac to return to the Washington area.

Washington, August 3, 1862—7.45 p.m.

It is determined to withdraw your army from the Peninsula to Aquia Creek. You will take immediate measures to effect this, covering the movement the best you can. Its real object and withdrawal should be concealed even from your own officers. Your material and transportation should be removed first. You will assume control of all the means of transportation within your reach, and apply to the naval forces for all the assistance they can render you. You will consult freely with the commander of these forces. The entire execution of the movement is left to your discretion and judgment.

You will leave such forces as you may deem proper at Fort Monroe, Norfolk, and other places, which we must occupy.

H. W. HALLECK,
Major-General, Commanding U.S. Army. [25]

The Army of the Potomac marched down the Peninsula from August 14 to August 19. Soldiers' return to northeast Virginia by water transport began on August 20. Union forces would not be in this part of Virginia, in any strength, until the late summer of 1864.

This completes your tour of the critical decisions.

If you wish to do an in-depth battlefield tour use Matt Spruill III and Matt Spruill IV, *Echoes of Thunder: A Guide to the Seven Days Battles* published by University of Tennessee Press

APPENDIX II

UNION ORDER OF BATTLE

ARMY OF THE POTOMAC
  Maj. Gen. George B. McClellan

SECOND CORPS
  Brig. Gen. Edwin V. Sumner

FIRST DIVISION
  Brig. Gen. Israel B. Richardson

FIRST BRIGADE
  Brig. Gen. John C. Caldwell
  5th New Hampshire
  61st New York
  81st Pennsylvania

SECOND BRIGADE
  Brig. Gen. Thomas F. Meagher
  29th Massachusetts
  63d New York
  69th New York
  88th New York

THIRD BRIGADE
Brig. Gen. William H. French
2d Delaware
52d New York
57th New York
64th New York
66th New York
53d Pennsylvania

ARTILLERY
Capt. George W. Hazzard
Battery B, 1st New York Artillery
Batteries A and C, 4th US Artillery

SECOND DIVISION
Brig. Gen. John Sedgwick

FIRST BRIGADE
Col. Alfred Sully
15th Massachusetts
1st Minnesota
34th New York
82d New York
1st Company Massachusetts Sharpshooters
2d Company Minnesota Sharpshooters

SECOND BRIGADE
Brig. Gen. William W. Burns (w)
69th Pennsylvania
71st Pennsylvania
72d Pennsylvania
106th Pennsylvania

THIRD BRIGADE
Brig. Gen. Napoleon J. T. Dana
19th Massachusetts
20th Massachusetts
7th Michigan
42d New York

ARTILLERY
Col. Charles H. Tompkins

Battery A, 1st Rhode Island Artillery
Battery I, 1st US Artillery

CORPS ARTILLERY RESERVE
Battery G, 1st New York Artillery
Battery B, 1st Rhode Island Artillery
Battery G, 1st Rhode Island Artillery

THIRD CORPS
Brig. Gen. Samuel P. Heintzelman

SECOND DIVISION
Brig. Gen. Joseph Hooker

FIRST BRIGADE
Brig. Gen. Cuvier Grover
1st Massachusetts
11th Massachusetts
16th Massachusetts
2d New Hampshire
26th Pennsylvania

SECOND BRIGADE
Brig. Gen. Daniel E. Sickles
70th New York
71st New York
72d New York
73d New York
74th New York

THIRD BRIGADE
Col. Joseph B. Carr
5th New Jersey
6th New Jersey
7th New Jersey
8th New Jersey
2d New York

ARTILLERY
Battery D, 1st New York Artillery
4th Battery, New York Artillery
Battery H, 1st US Artillery

THIRD DIVISION
Brig. Gen. Phillip Kearny

FIRST BRIGADE
Brig. Gen. John C. Robinson
20th Indiana
87th New York
57th Pennsylvania
63d Pennsylvania
105th Pennsylvania

SECOND BRIGADE
Brig. Gen. David B. Birney
3d Maine
4th Maine
38th New York
40th New York
101st New York

THIRD BRIGADE
Brig. Gen. Hiram G. Berry
2d Michigan
3d Michigan
5th Michigan
1st New York
37th New York

ARTILLERY
Battery E, 1st Rhode Island Artillery
Battery G, 2d US Artillery

CORPS ARTILLERY RESERVE
Capt. Gustavus A. DeRussy
6th Battery, New York Artillery
2d Battery, New Jersey Artillery
Battery K, 4th US Artillery

FOURTH CORPS
Brig. Gen. Erasmus D. Keyes

FIRST DIVISION
Brig. Gen. Darius N. Couch

FIRST BRIGADE
Brig. Gen. Albion P. Howe
55th New York
62d New York
93d Pennsylvania
98th Pennsylvania
102d Pennsylvania

SECOND BRIGADE
Brig. Gen. John J. Abercrombie
65th New York
67th New York
23d Pennsylvania
31st Pennsylvania
61st Pennsylvania

THIRD BRIGADE
Brig. Gen. Innis N. Palmer
7th Massachusetts
10th Massachusetts
36th New York
2d Rhode Island

ARTILLERY
Battery C, 1st Pennsylvania Artillery
Battery D, 1st Pennsylvania Artillery

SECOND DIVISION
Brig. Gen. John J. Peck

FIRST BRIGADE
Brig. Gen. Henry M. Naglee
11th Maine
56th New York
100th New York
52d Pennsylvania
104th Pennsylvania

SECOND BRIGADE
Brig. Gen. Henry W. Wessells
81st New York
85th New York

92d New York
96th New York
98th New York
85th Pennsylvania
101st Pennsylvania
103d Pennsylvania

ARTILLERY
Battery H, 1st New York Artillery
7th Battery, New York Artillery

CORPS ARTILLERY RESERVE
Maj. Robert M. West
8th Battery, New York Artillery
Battery E, 1st Pennsylvania Artillery
Battery H, 1st Pennsylvania Artillery
Battery M, 5th US Artillery

FIFTH CORPS
Brig. Gen. Fitz John Porter

FIRST DIVISION
Brig. Gen. George W. Morell

FIRST BRIGADE
Brig. Gen. John H. Martindale
2d Maine
22d Massachusetts
1st Michigan
13th New York
25th New York
2d Company Massachusetts Sharpshooters

SECOND BRIGADE
Brig. Gen. Charles Griffin
9th Massachusetts
4th Michigan
14th New York
62d Pennsylvania

THIRD BRIGADE
Brig. Gen. Daniel Butterfield

12th New York
44th New York
16th Michigan
83d Pennsylvania
Brady's Company Michigan Sharpshooters

ARTILLERY
Capt. William B. Weeden
3d (C) Battery, Massachusetts Artillery
5th (E) Battery Massachusetts Artillery
Battery C, 1st Rhode Island Artillery
Battery D, 5th US Artillery

SHARPSHOOTERS
1st US Sharpshooters

SECOND DIVISION
Brig. Gen. George Sykes

FIRST BRIGADE
Col. Robert C. Buchanan
3d US Infantry
4th US Infantry
12th US Infantry
14th US Infantry

SECOND BRIGADE
Lieut. Col. William Chapman
Maj. Charles S. Lovell
2d US Infantry
6th US Infantry
10th US Infantry
11th U. S Infantry
17th US Infantry

THIRD BRIGADE
Col. Gouverneur K. Warren
5th New York
10th New York

ARTILLERY
Capt. Stephen H. Weed

Batteries L and M, 3d US Artillery
Battery I, 5th US Artillery

THIRD DIVISION
Brig. Gen. George A. McCall
Brig. Gen. Truman Seymour

FIRST BRIGADE
Brig. Gen. John F. Reynolds
Col. Seneca G. Simmons
Col. R. Biddle Roberts
1st Pennsylvania Reserves
2d Pennsylvania Reserves
5th Pennsylvania Reserves
8th Pennsylvania Reserves
13th Pennsylvania Reserves

SECOND BRIGADE
Brig. Gen. George G. Meade
Col. Albert L. Magilton
3d Pennsylvania Reserves
4th Pennsylvania Reserves
7th Pennsylvania Reserves
11th Pennsylvania Reserves

THIRD BRIGADE
Brig. Gen. Truman Seymour
Col. C. Feger Jackson
9th Pennsylvania Reserves
10th Pennsylvania Reserves
12th Pennsylvania Reserves

ARTILLERY
Battery A, 1st Pennsylvania Artillery
Battery B, 1st Pennsylvania Artillery
Battery G, 1st Pennsylvania Artillery
Battery C, 5th US Artillery

SIXTH CORPS
Brig. Gen. William B. Franklin

FIRST DIVISION
   Brig. Gen. Henry W. Slocum

FIRST BRIGADE
   Brig. Gen. George W. Taylor
   1st New Jersey
   2d New Jersey
   3d New Jersey
   4th New Jersey

SECOND BRIGADE
   Col. Joseph J. Bartlett
   5th Maine
   16th New York
   27th New York
   96th Pennsylvania

THIRD BRIGADE
   Brig. Gen. John Newton
   18th New York
   31st New York
   32d New York
   95th Pennsylvania

ARTILLERY
   Capt. Edward R. Platt
   1st Battery, Massachusetts Artillery
   1st Battery, New Jersey Artillery
   Battery D, 2d US Artillery

SECOND DIVISION
   Brig. Gen. William F. Smith

FIRST BRIGADE
   Brig. Gen. Winfield W. Hancock
   6th Maine
   43d New York
   49th Pennsylvania
   5th Wisconsin

SECOND BRIGADE
   Brig. Gen. William T. H. Brooks

2d Vermont
3d Vermont
5th Vermont
6th Vermont

THIRD BRIGADE
Brig. Gen. John W. Davidson
7th Maine
20th New York
33d New York
49th New York
77th New York

ARTILLERY
Capt. Romeyn B. Ayres
Battery E, 1st New York Artillery
1st Battery, New York Artillery
3d Battery, New York Artillery
Battery F, 5th US Artillery

ARMY ARTILLERY RESERVE
Col. Henry J. Hunt

FIRST BRIGADE
(Horse Artillery)
Lieut. Col. William Hays
Battery A, 2d US Artillery
Batteries B and L, 2d US Artillery
Battery M, 2d Artillery

SECOND BRIGADE
Lieut. Col. George W. Getty
Batteries E and G, 1st US Artillery
Battery K, 1st US Artillery
Battery G, 4th US Artillery
Battery A, 5th US Artillery
Battery K, 5th US Artillery

THIRD BRIGADE
Maj. Albert Arndt
Battery A, 1st Battalion, New York Artillery
Battery B, 1st Battalion, New York Artillery

Battery C, 1st Battalion, New York Artillery
Battery D, 1st Battalion, New York Artillery

FOURTH BRIGADE
Maj. Edward R. Petherbridge
Battery A, Maryland Artillery
Battery B, Maryland Artillery

FIFTH BRIGADE
Capt. J. Howard Carlisle
Battery E, 2d US Artillery
Batteries F and K, 3d US Artillery

SIEGE TRAIN
Col. Robert O. Tyler
1st Connecticut Heavy Artillery

ARMY CAVALRY RESERVE
Brig. Gen. Phillip St. George Cooke

FIRST BRIGADE
Brig. Gen. William H. Emory
6th Pennsylvania Cavalry
5th US Cavalry (5 Companies)

SECOND BRIGADE
Col. George A. H. Blake
1st US Cavalry (4 Companies)
6th US Cavalry (Detached)

VOLUNTEER ENGINEER BRIGADE
Brig. Gen. Daniel P. Woodbury
15th New York Engineers
50th New York Engineers
Battalion US Engineers

CASEY'S COMMAND AT WHITE HOUSE LANDING
Brig. Gen. Silas Casey
4th Pennsylvania Cavalry (Squadron)
11th Pennsylvania Cavalry (5 Companies)
93d New York (6 Companies)
Battery F, 1st New York Artillery
Batteries C and G, 3d US Artillery

[US War Department, *The War of the Rebellion: A Compilation of the Official Records of the Union and Confederate Armies* (Washington, DC: US Government Printing Office, 1880–1901), ser. 1, vol. 11, pt. 2, pp. 24–37 and Robert U. Johnson and Clarence C. Buel, eds., *Battles and Leaders of the Civil War: Being for the Most Part Contributions by Union and Confederate Officers* (1884; repr., Secaucus, NJ: Castle Books, 1982), 2:313–15.]

APPENDIX III

CONFEDERATE ORDER OF BATTLE

ARMY OF NORTHERN VIRGINIA
  Gen. Robert E. Lee

JACKSON'S COMMAND
  Maj. Gen. Thomas J. Jackson

WHITING'S DIVISION
  Brig. Gen. William H. C. Whiting

HOOD'S BRIGADE
  Brig. Gen. John B. Hood
  18th Georgia
  1st Texas
  4th Texas
  5th Texas
  Hampton Legion

LAW'S BRIGADE
  Col. Evander M. Law
  4th Alabama
  2d Mississippi
  11th Mississippi
  6th North Carolina

ARTILLERY
Balthis's Battery, Staunton (VA) Artillery
Reilly's Battery, Rowan (NC) Artillery

JACKSON'S DIVISION
Brig. Gen. Charles S. Winder

WINDER'S BRIGADE
Brig. Gen. Charles S. Winder
2d Virginia
4th Virginia
5th Virginia
27th Virginia
33d Virginia
Carpenter's (VA) Battery
Poague's Battery, Rockbridge (VA) Artillery

JONES'S BRIGADE
Brig. Gen. J. R. Jones
Lieut. Col. R. H. Cunningham Jr.
21st Virginia
42d Virginia
48th Virginia
1st Virginia Battalion (Irish)
Caskie's Battery, Hampden (VA) Artillery

FULKERSON'S BRIGADE
Col. S. V. Fulkerson
Col. E. T. H. Warren
Brig. Gen. Wade Hampton
10th Virginia
23d Virginia
37th Virginia
Wooding's Battery, Danville (VA) Artillery

LAWTON'S BRIGADE
Brig. Gen. Alexander R. Lawton
13th Georgia
26th Georgia
31st Georgia
38th Georgia
60th Georgia
61st Georgia

EWELL'S DIVISION
Maj. Gen. Richard S. Ewell

ELZEY'S BRIGADE
Brig. Gen. Arnold Elzey
Col. James A. Walker
Brig. Gen. Jubal A. Early
12th Georgia
13th Virginia
25th Virginia
31st Virginia
44th Virginia
52d Virginia
58th Virginia

TRIMBLE'S BRIGADE
Brig. Gen. Isaac R. Trimble
15th Alabama
21st Georgia
16th Mississippi
21st North Carolina
1st North Carolina Battalion
Courtney's (VA) Battery

TAYLOR'S BRIGADE
Brig. Gen. Richard Taylor
Col. I. G. Seymour
Col. Leroy A. Stafford
6th Louisiana
7th Louisiana
8th Louisiana
9th Louisiana
1st Louisiana Special Battalion
Carrington's Battery, Charlottesville (VA) Artillery

MARYLAND LINE
Col. Bradley T. Johnson
1st Maryland
Brockenbrough's Battery, Baltimore (MD) Artillery

D. H. HILL'S DIVISION
Maj. Gen. Daniel H. Hill

RODES'S BRIGADE
  Brig. Gen. Robert E. Rodes
  Col. John B. Gordon
  3d Alabama
  5th Alabama
  6th Alabama
  12th Alabama
  26th Alabama
  Carter's Battery, King William (VA) Artillery

G. B. ANDERSON'S BRIGADE
  Brig. Gen. George B. Anderson
  Col. C. C. Tew
  2d North Carolina
  4th North Carolina
  14th North Carolina
  30th North Carolina
  Hardaway's (Alabama) Battery

GARLAND'S BRIGADE
  Brig. Gen. Samuel Garland
  5th North Carolina
  12th North Carolina
  13th North Carolina
  20th North Carolina
  23d North Carolina
  Bondurant's Battery, Jeff. Davis (AL) Artillery

COLQUITT'S BRIGADE
  Col. Alfred H. Colquitt
  13th Alabama
  6th Georgia
  23d Georgia
  27th Georgia
  28th Georgia, Col. T. J. Warthen
  Nelson's Battery, Hanover (VA) Artillery

RIPLEY'S BRIGADE
  Brig. Gen. Roswell S. Ripley
  44th Georgia
  48th Georgia
  1st North Carolina
  3d North Carolina

JONES'S ARTILLERY BATTALION
Maj. Hilary P. Jones
Clark's (VA) Battery
Peyton's Battery, Orange (VA) Artillery
Rhett's (SC) Battery

MAGRUDER'S COMMAND
Maj. Gen. John B. Magruder

FIRST DIVISION
Brig. Gen. David R. Jones

TOOMBS'S BRIGADE
Brig. Gen. Robert Toombs
2nd Georgia
15th Georgia
17th Georgia
20th Georgia

G. T. ANDERSON'S BRIGADE
Col. George T. Anderson
1st Georgia (Regulars)
7th Georgia
8th Georgia
9th Georgia
11th Georgia

ARTILLERY
Maj. John J. Garnett
Brown's Battery, Wise (VA) Artillery
Hart's Battery, Washington (SC) Artillery
Lane's (GA) Battery
Moody's (LA) Battery
Woolfolk's Battery, Ashland (VA) Artillery

McLAWS'S DIVISION
Maj. Gen. Lafayette McLaws

SEMMES'S BRIGADE
Brig. Gen. Paul J. Semmes
10th Georgia

53d Georgia
5th Louisiana
10th Louisiana
15th Virginia
32d Virginia
Manly's (NC) Battery

KERSHAW'S BRIGADE
Brig. Gen. Joseph B. Kershaw
2d South Carolina
3d South Carolina
7th South Carolina
8th South Carolina
Kemper's Battery, Alexandria (VA) Artillery

MAGRUDER'S DIVISION
Maj. Gen. John B. Magruder

COBB'S BRIGADE
Brig. Gen. Howell Cobb
16th Georgia
24th Georgia
Cobb (GA) Legion
2d Louisiana
15th North Carolina
Troup (GA) Artillery

GRIFFITH'S BRIGADE
Brig. Gen. Richard Griffith
Col. William Barksdale
13th Mississippi
17th Mississippi
18th Mississippi
21st Mississippi
McCarthy's (VA) Battery

ARTILLERY
Col. Stephen D. Lee
Kirkpatrick's Battery, Amherst (VA) Artillery
Page's Battery, Magruder (VA) Artillery
Read's Battery, Pulaski (GA) Artillery
Richardson's Battery

LONGSTREET'S DIVISION
Maj. Gen. James Longstreet

KEMPER'S BRIGADE
Brig. Gen. James L. Kemper
1st Virginia
7th Virginia
11th Virginia
17th Virginia
24th Virginia
Rogers's (VA) Battery

R. H. ANDERSON'S BRIGADE
Brig. Gen. Richard H. Anderson
Col. Micah Jenkins
2d South Carolina Rifles
4th South Carolina
5th South Carolina
6th South Carolina
Palmetto (SC) Sharpshooters

PICKETT'S BRIGADE
Brig. Gen. George E. Pickett
Col. Eppa Hunton
Col. John B. Strange
8th Virginia
18th Virginia
19th Virginia
28th Virginia
56th Virginia

WILCOX'S BRIGADE
Brig. Gen. Cadmus M. Wilcox
8th Alabama
9th Alabama
10th Alabama
11th Alabama
Anderson's Battery, Thomas (VA) Artillery

PRYOR'S BRIGADE
Brig. Gen. Roger A. Pryor
14th Alabama
2d Florida

14th Louisiana
1st Louisiana Battalion
3d Virginia
Maurin's Battery, Donaldsonville (LA) Artillery

FEATHERSTON'S BRIGADE
Brig. Gen. Winfield S. Featherston
12th Mississippi
19th Mississippi
2d Mississippi Battalion
Smith's Battery, 3d Richmond Howitzers

ARTILLERY
Washington (LA) Battalion
Dearing's Battery (Lynchburg, VA)
Chapman's Battery (Dixie Artillery)

HUGER'S DIVISION
Maj. Gen. Benjamin Huger

MAHONE'S BRIGADE
Brig. Gen. William Mahone
6th Virginia
12th Virginia
16th Virginia
41st Virginia
49th Virginia
Grimes's (VA) Battery
Moorman's (VA) Battery

WRIGHT'S BRIGADE
Brig. Gen. Ambrose R. Wright
44th Alabama
3d Georgia
4th Georgia
22d Georgia
1st Louisiana
Huger's (VA) Battery
Ross's (GA) Battery

ARMISTEAD'S BRIGADE
Brig. Gen. Lewis A. Armistead
9th Virginia

14th Virginia
38th Virginia
53d Virginia
57th Virginia
5th Virginia Battalion
Stribling's Battery, Fauquier (VA) Artillery
Turner's (VA) Battery

RANSOM'S BRIGADE (ATTACHED)
Brig. Gen. Robert Ransom Jr.
24th North Carolina
25th North Carolina
26th North Carolina
35th North Carolina
48th North Carolina
49th North Carolina

A. P. HILL'S (LIGHT) DIVISION
Maj. Gen. Ambrose P. Hill

FIELD'S BRIGADE
Brig. Gen. Charles W. Field
40th Virginia
47th Virginia
55th Virginia
60th Virginia

GREGG'S BRIGADE
Brig. Gen. Maxcy Gregg
1st South Carolina
1st South Carolina Rifles
12th South Carolina
13th South Carolina
14th South Carolina

J. R. ANDERSON'S BRIGADE
Brig. Gen. Joseph R. Anderson
Col. Edward L. Thomas
14th Georgia
35th Georgia
45th Georgia
49th Georgia
3d Louisiana Battalion

BRANCH'S BRIGADE
Brig. Gen. Lawrence O'B. Branch
7th North Carolina
18th North Carolina
28th North Carolina
33d North Carolina
37th North Carolina

ARCHER'S BRIGADE
Brig. Gen. James J. Archer
5th Alabama Battalion
19th Georgia
1st Tennessee
7th Tennessee
14th Tennessee

PENDER'S BRIGADE
Brig. Gen. William D. Pender
2d Arkansas Battalion
16th North Carolina
22d North Carolina
34th North Carolina
38th North Carolina
22d Virginia Battalion

ARTILLERY
Lieut. Col. Lewis M. Coleman
Andrews's (MD) Battery
Bachman's (SC) Battery
Braxton's Battery, Fredericksburg (VA) Artillery
Crenshaw's (VA) Battery
Davidson's Battery, Letcher (VA) Artillery
Johnson's (VA) Battery
McIntosh's Battery, Pee Dee (SC) Artillery
Purcell (VA) Battery

HOLMES'S DIVISION
Maj. Gen. Theophilus H. Holmes

DANIEL'S BRIGADE
Brig. Gen. Junius Daniel

43d North Carolina
45th North Carolina
50th North Carolina
Burroughs's Battalion (Cavalry)

WALKER'S BRIGADE
Brig. Gen. John G. Walker
Col. Van H. Manning
3d Arkansas
2d Georgia Battalion
27th North Carolina
46th North Carolina
30th Virginia
Goodwyn's Cavalry Company

ARTILLERY
Col. James Deshler
Branch's (VA) Battery
Brem's (NC) Battery
French's (VA) Battery
Graham's (VA) Battery
Grandy's (VA) Battery
Lloyd's (NC) Battery

WISE'S COMMAND
(Attached to Holmes's Division)
Brig. Gen. Henry A. Wise
26th Virginia
46th Virginia
Andrews's (VA) Battery
Armistead's (VA) Battery
French's (VA) Battery
Rives's (VA) Battery

RESERVE ARTILLERY
Brig. Gen. William N. Pendleton

FIRST VIRGINIA ARTILLERY
Col. J. Thompson Brown
Coke's Williamsburg (VA) Battery

Macon's Battery
Richardson's Battery
Watson's Battery

JONES'S BATTALION
Attached to D. H. Hill's Division
Maj. H. P. Jones

NELSON'S BATTALON
Maj. William Nelson
Huckstep's (VA) Battery
Page's (VA) Battery

RICHARDSON'S BATTALION
Maj. Charles Richardson
Ancell's (VA) Battery
Milledge's (GA) Battery
Masters' (VA) Battery

SUMTER (GA) BATTALION
Lieut. Col. A. S. Cutts
Blackshear's (GA) Battery
Price's (GA) Battery
Hamilton's (GA) Battery

CAVALRY
Brig. Gen. James E. B. Stuart
1st North Carolina
1st Virginia
3d Virginia
4th Virginia
5th Virginia
9th Virginia
10th Virginia
Cobb (GA) Legion
Critcher's (VA) Battalion
Hampton's (SC) Legion
Jeff. Davis (MS) Legion
Stuart Horse Artillery

[US War Department, *The War of the Rebellion: A Compilation of the Official Records of the Union and Confederate Armies* (Washington, DC: US Government Printing Office, 1880–1901), ser. 1, vol. 11, pt. 2, pp. 483–89 and Robert U. Johnson and Clarence C. Buel, eds., *Battles and Leaders of the Civil War: Being for the Most Part Contributions by Union and Confederate Officers* (1884; repr., Secaucus, NJ: Castle Books, 1982), 2:315–17.]

NOTES

Introduction

1. Mark Boatner III, *The Civil War Dictionary* (New York: David McKay, 1959), 932, 148–49, 907–8; William C. Davis, *First Blood: Fort Sumner to Bull Run* (Alexandria, VA: Time-Life Books, 1983), 155.

2. Thomas Lawrence Connelly, *Army of the Heartland: The Army of Tennessee, 1861–1862* (Baton Rouge: Louisiana State University Press, 1967), 99; James R. Knight, *The Battle of Pea Ridge: The Civil War Fight for the Ozarks* (Charleston, SC: History Press, 2012), 136.

3. US War Department, *The War of the Rebellion: A Compilation of the Official Records of the Union and Confederate Armies* (Washington, DC: US Government Printing Office, 1880–1901), ser. 1, vol. 9, pp. 506–12, 530–35, 540–45, 551. (Hereafter cited as *OR*, followed by appropriate volume, part, and page numbers. All citations are from series 1 unless otherwise noted.)

4. Boatner, *Civil War Dictionary*, 394–97, 752–57; Timothy B. Smith, *Shiloh: Conquer or Perish* (Lawrence: University Press of Kansas, 2014), 401–2; Brian K. Burton, *Extraordinary Circumstances: The Seven Days Battles* (Bloomington: Indiana University Press, 2001), 1–2; Robert A. Doughty and Charles F. Brower IV, *The West Point Atlas of American Wars, Volume I: 1689–1900*, rev. and updated ed. (New York: Henry Holt, 1995), 31.

5. Burton, *Extraordinary Circumstances*, 2; Allan Nevins, *The War for the Union: War Becomes Revolution 1862–1863*, 2 vols. (New York: Charles Scribner's Sons, 1960): vol. number: 2–90.

6. Joseph L. Harsh, *Confederate Tide Rising: Robert E. Lee and the Making of Southern Strategy, 1861–1862* (Kent, OH: Kent State University Press, 1998), 27–28.

7. *OR*, vol. 12, pt. 3, p. 435; Peter Cozzens, *General John Pope: A Life for the Nation* (Urbana: University of Illinois Press, 2000), 75–76; Harsh, *Confederate Tide Rising*, 35.

8. James M. McPherson, *Battle Cry of Freedom: The Civil War Era* (New York: Oxford University Press, 1988), 363–64, 489, 500; Nevins, *War for the Union*, vol. number 2-144, 146; David Herbert Donald, *Lincoln* (London: Jonathan Cape Random House, 1995), 365.

Chapter 1

1. Spruill. A turning movement avoids an enemy's main defensive position by seizing objectives deep in the opponent's rear area. Doing so causes the enemy to move out of its current position or divert major forces against the new threat. The presence of a friendly force in its rear area turns an opponent out of its position.

2. Ezra J. Warner, *Generals in Blue: Lives of the Union Commanders* (Baton Rouge: Louisiana State University Press, 1964), 290–91.

3. Stephen W. Sears, *Lincoln's Lieutenants: The High Command of the Army of the Potomac* (Boston: Houghton Mifflin Harcourt, 2017), 113–15, 126; Stephen W. Sears, *To the Gates of Richmond: The Peninsula Campaign* (New York: Ticknor and Fields, 1992), 3–4.

4. Boatner, *Civil War Dictionary*, 664, 738–39.

5. Sears, *To the Gates of Richmond*, 14; Doughty and Brower, *West Point Atlas, Volume I*, 39.

6. George B. McClellan, "The Peninsula Campaign," in *Battles and Leaders of the Civil War: Being for the Most Part Contributions by Union and Confederate Officers*, ed. Robert U. Johnson and Clarence C. Buel, (1884; repr., Secaucus, NJ: Castle Books, 1982), 2:168; Sears, *To the Gates of Richmond*, 23–24; William F. Miller, comp., "The Grand Campaign: A Journal of Operations on the Peninsula, March 17–August 26, 1862," in *The Peninsula Campaign of 1862: Yorktown to the Seven Days*, ed. William J. Miller (Campbell, CA: Savas-Woodbury, 1993), 1:205.

7. Miller, "Grand Campaign," 1:186; Doughty and Brower, *West Point Atlas, Volume I*, 40; Sears, *To the Gates of Richmond*, 29–30; John C. Palfrey, "The Siege of Yorktown," in *Papers of the Military Historical Society of Massachusetts*, vol. 1, *Campaigns in Virginia, 1861–1862*, ed. Theodore F. Dwight (1895; repr., Wilmington, NC: Broadfoot, 1989), 98.

8. Sears, *To the Gates of Richmond*, 26; Ezra J. Warner, *Generals in Gray: Lives of the Confederate Commanders* (Baton Rouge: Louisiana State University Press, 1959), 207.

9. Doughty and Brower, *West Point Atlas, Volume I*, 40; Alexander S. Webb, *The Peninsula: McClellan's Campaign of 1862* (1881; repr., Wilmington, NC: Broadfoot, 1989), 49; Sears, *To the Gates of Richmond*, 26.

10 Sears, *To the Gates of Richmond*, 36, 37–38.

11. Webb, *Peninsula*, 43, 56–57; Sears, *To the Gates of Richmond*, 35; Doughty and Brower, *West Point Atlas, Volume I*, 40; *OR*, 5, 19; Edward G. Longacre, *The Man behind the Guns: A Biography of General Henry J. Hunt, Commander of Artillery, Army of the Potomac* (South Brunswick, NJ: A. S. Barnes, 1977), 108.

12. Sears, *To the Gates of Richmond*, 35, 36–37; Miller, "Grand Campaign," 1:183; William Swinton, *Campaigns of the Army of the Potomac* (Secaucus, NJ: Blue and Gray, 1988), 101.

13. *OR*, vol. 11, pt. 1, p. 339.

14. Webb, *Peninsula*, 59–60; *OR*, vol. 11, pt. 1, pp. 339–48.

15. Jubal A. Early, *General Jubal A. Early: Autobiographical Sketch and Narrative of the War between the States* (1912; repr., Wilmington, NC: Broadfoot, 1989), 56–57; *OR*, vol. 11, pt. 1, p. 601; Webb, *Peninsula*, 60; Miller, "Grand Campaign," 1:186.

16. Sears, *To the Gates of Richmond*, 8, 19, 34; *OR*, vol. 11, pt. 3, pp. 60–62.

17. *OR*, vol. 11, pt. 1, p. 28; *OR*, vol. 11, pt. 3, pp. 53, 66, 177; Sears, *To the Gates of Richmond*, 41, 45, 97; Doughty and Brower, *West Point Atlas, Volume I*, 51.

18. Robert G. Tanner, *Stonewall in the Valley: Thomas J. "Stonewall" Jackson's Shenandoah Valley Campaign, Spring 1862* (Mechanicsburg, PA: Stackpole Books, 1996), 234, 327.

19. *OR*, vol. 12, pt. 3, p. 219.

20. *OR*, vol. 12, pt. 3, pp. 220, 231; *OR*, vol. 12, pt. 1, p. 12; Doughty and Brower, *West Point Atlas, Volume I*, 53; Tanner, *Stonewall in the Valley*, 345.

21. Matt Spruill III and Matt Spruill IV, *Decisions at Second Manassas: The*

Fourteen Critical Decisions That Defined the Battle (Knoxville: University of Tennessee Press, 2018), 8, 13, 113.

22. Miller, "Grand Campaign," 1:186; Sears, *To the Gates of Richmond*, 85.

23. Miller, "Grand Campaign," 187, 188; Sears, *To the Gates of Richmond*, 93–94.

24. Ronald H. Bailey, *Forward to Richmond: McClellan's Peninsula Campaign* (Alexandria, VA: Time-Life Books, 1983), 91; Miller, "Grand Campaign," 1:189.

25. Warner, *Generals in Gray*, 161–62.

26. Bailey, *Forward to Richmond*, 136–56; Sears, *To the Gates of Richmond*, 118–19, 121–24, 133, 138–40.

27. William C. Davis, *Jefferson C. Davis: The Man and His Hour* (New York, NY: Harper-Collins Publishers, 1991), 6, 37, 39, 49, 132–39, 152–60, 173, 215, 222, 303, 635–37, 656–57, 669, 687–88.

28. Warner, *Generals in Gray*, 280–81; Sears, *To the Gates of Richmond*, 141.

29. In order of seniority they were: Samuel Cooper, Albert Sidney Johnston, Robert E. Lee, Joseph E. Johnston, and P. G. T. Beauregard. Later in the war Braxton Bragg and Edmund Kirby Smith were also promoted to this rank. John B. Hood was promoted to general by Jefferson Davis, but it was never confirmed by the Confederate Congress.

30. Warner, *Generals in Gray*, 180–82; Steven E. Woodward, *Davis and Lee at War* (Lawrence: University Press of Kansas, 1995), 148.

31. Warner, *Generals in Gray*, 180–82; Woodward, *Davis and Lee at War*, 148.

32. James A. Kegel, *North with Lee and Jackson: The Lost Story of Gettysburg* (Mechanicsburg, PA: Stackpole Books, 1996), 99–100; Doughty and Brower, *West Point Atlas, Volume I*, 49–53.

33. Doughty and Brower, *West Point Atlas, Volume I*, 43; Judkin Browning, *The Seven Days' Battles: The War Begins Anew* (Santa Barbara, CA: Praeger, 2012), 26.

34. Kegel, *North with Lee and Jackson*, 99–100.

35. Harsh, *Confederate Tide Rising*, 28, 36.

36. Kegel, *North with Lee and Jackson*, 102–3.

37. Sears, *To the Gates of Richmond*, 153; Doughty and Brower, *West Point Atlas, Volume I*, 39.

38. There are five forms of maneuver that can be used when conducting an attack: envelopment, turning movement, infiltration, penetration, and frontal attack. An attacking force uses a turning movement to avoid the

enemy's principal defensive position by seizing objectives in the enemy rear and causing him to move out of his current position or divert major forces against a new threat.

39. Whiting's Division was sent to reinforce Jackson and replaced with Mc-Laws's and D. R. Jones's Divisions. Longstreet's and D. H. Hill's Divisions were pulled out of line and sent to the left to be part of the turning movement. Armistead L. Long, *Memoirs of Robert E. Lee: His Military and Personal History* (1886; repr., Secaucus, NJ: Blue and Gray, 1983), 164.

40. Fitz John Porter, "Hanover Court House and Gaines Mill," in *Battles and Leaders of the Civil War: Being for the Most Part Contributions by Union and Confederate Officers*, ed. Robert U. Johnson and Clarence C. Buel (1884; repr., Secaucus, NJ: Castle Books, 1982), 2:325; Browning, *The Seven Days' Battles*, 30, 35–36, 41; Burton, *Extraordinary Circumstances*, 5; William F. Miller, comp., "Logistics, Friction and McClellan's Strategy for the Peninsula Campaign" in *The Peninsula Campaign of 1862: Yorktown to the Seven Days*, ed. William J. Miller (Campbell, CA: Savas-Woodbury, 1993), 2:136, 160.

41. Matt Spruill III and Matt Spruill IV, *Echoes of Thunder: A Guide to the Seven Days Battles* (Knoxville: University of Tennessee Press, 2006), 7.

42. Frederick Maurice, *An Aide de Camp of Robert E. Lee: Being the Papers of Colonel Charles Marshall* (Boston: Little, Brown, 1927), 82.

43. Maurice, *Aide de Camp of Robert E. Lee*, 86–87; Long, *Memoirs of Robert E. Lee*, 170; Douglas S. Freeman, *Lee's Lieutenants: A Study in Command*, vol. 1, *Manassas to Malvern Hill* (New York: Charles Scribner's Sons, 1942), 497.

44. Lenoir Chambers, *Stonewall Jackson*, vol. 2, *Seven Days to the Last March* (1959, repr., Wilmington, NC: Broadfoot, 1988), 2:9–11; Spruill and Spruill, *Decisions at Second Manassas*, 104–5.

45. Matthew Forney Steele, *American Campaigns* (Washington, DC: Byron S. Adams, 1909), 204; Long, *Memoirs of Robert E. Lee*, 170.

46. Freeman, *Lee's Lieutenants*, 1:495; Steele, *American Campaigns*, 203.

Chapter 2

1. *OR*, vol. 11, pt. 1, pp. 31, 38–39, 53, 162, 273; Browning, *The Seven Days' Battles*, 41.

2. Robert E. Lee to Jefferson Davis, June 5, 1862, in Douglas S. Freeman, *Lee's Dispatches: Unpublished Letters of Robert E. Lee to Jefferson Davis*

(1915; repr., Baton Rouge: Louisiana State University Press, 1994), 6–7; Spruill and Spruill, *Echoes of Thunder*, 5; *OR*, vol. 11, pt. 3, pp. 571–72, 573.

3. *OR*, vol. 11, pt. 2, pp. 489–90, 498–99; Browning, *The Seven Days' Battles*, 34–35; Spruill and Spruill, *Echoes of Thunder*, 14.

4. Warner, *Generals in Gray*, 134–35.

5. Chambers, *Stonewall Jackson*, 2:19, 20, 21.

6. Clifford Dowdey, *The Seven Days: The Emergence of Robert E. Lee* (1964; repr., Wilmington, NC: Broadfoot, 1988), 155.

7. Chambers, *Stonewall Jackson*, 2:24, 29, 33, 35–36.

8. "Complete Sun and Moon Date for One Day," US Naval Observatory Astronomical Applications Department website, http://aa.usno.navy.mil/index.php.

9. *OR*, vol. 11, pt. 2, p. 835; Burton, *Extraordinary Circumstances*, 66.

10. Warner, *Generals in Blue*, 378–80.

11. Warner, *Generals in Blue*, 378–80.

12. *OR*, vol. 11, pt. 2, pp. 222, 271, 384, 647, 897, 841, 835, 899; Spruill and Spruill, *Echoes of Thunder*, 21–43; Steven E. Woodworth, *Davis and Lee at War* (Lawrence: University Press of Kansas, 1995), 163.

13. *OR*, vol. 1, pt. 2, p. 223; Browning, *The Seven Days' Battles*, 57, 60; Richard A. Sauers, "The Pennsylvania Reserves," in *The Peninsula Campaign of 1862: Yorktown to the Seven Days*, ed. William J. Miller (Campbell, CA: Savas-Woodbury, 1993), 1:30; Sears, *To the Gates of Richmond*, 213, 214; Porter, "Hanover Court House and Gaines Mill," 2:334.

14. Browning, *Seven Days' Battles*, 62; Sears, *To the Gates of Richmond*, 219; Clifford Dowdey, *Seven Days*, 206.

15. *OR*, vol. 11, pt. 2, pp. 492–93; Browning, *The Seven Days' Battles*, 64–65; Sears, *To the Gates of Richmond*, 221, 223.

16. *OR*, vol. 11, pt. 2, pp. 491–92.

17. *OR*, vol. 11, pt. 2, pp. 492–93.

18. *OR*, vol. 11, pt. 2, pp. 222–23, 224–25.

19. Spruill and Spruill, *Echoes of Thunder*, 132; *OR*, vol. 11, pt. 1, p. 170.

20. Steele, *American Campaigns*, 206.

21. Browning, *The Seven Days' Battles*, 82–83.

Chapter 3

1. *OR*, vol. 11, pt. 2, p. 226; Sears, *To the Gates of Richmond*, 255, 259.

2. Spruill and Spruill, *Echoes of Thunder*, 132; *OR*, vol. 11, pt. 1, 170.

3. *OR*, vol. 11, pt. 2, pp. 515–17, 607; Browning, *The Seven Days' Battles*, 88; Robert E. Lee to Jefferson Davis, June 29, 1862, in *The Wartime Papers of Robert E. Lee*, ed. Clifford Dowdey and Louis H. Manarin (1961; repr., Da Capo), 205–6.

4. The four types of offensive operations are movement to contact, attack, pursuit, and exploitation.

5. Freeman, *Lee's Lieutenants*, 1:565–66.

6. Ewell's Division had been detached and sent to Bottoms Bridge.

7. Spruill and Spruill, *Echoes of Thunder*, 133–34; *OR*, vol. 11, pt. 2, pp. 494–95; Burton, *Extraordinary Circumstances*, 236.

8. Spruill and Spruill, *Echoes of Thunder*, 133–34.

9. Freeman, *Lee's Lieutenants*, 1:566.

10. Sears, *Lincoln's Lieutenants*, 255–58; *OR*, vol. 11, pt. 2, pp. 494–95.

11. An overgrown farm road that paralleled the Willis Church Road was discovered, cleared of brush and was used by part of the supply train.

12. D. H. Hill's Division was attached and Ewell's Division was detached.

13. Spruill and Spruill, *Echoes of Thunder*, 153–54; *OR*, vol. 11, pt. 2, pp. 55, 431.

14. *OR*, vol. 11, pt. 2, pp. 561, 627; Browning, *Seven Days' Battles*, 111.

15. Browning, *The Seven Days' Battles*, 111–12; Freeman, *Lee's Lieutenants*, 1:599, 576–79.

16. *OR*, vol. 11, pt. 2, pp. 92–93, 94–95.

17. Browning, *The Seven Days' Battles*, 105–8; Spruill and Spruill, *Echoes of Thunder*, 157–242.

18. Warner, *Generals in Gray*, 143–44.

19. Spruill and Spruill, *Echoes of Thunder*, 133–34; *OR*, vol. 11, pt. 2, pp. 494–95.

20. Browning, *The Seven Days' Battles*, 110; Freeman, *Lee's Lieutenants*, 1:567; Dowdey, *Seven Days*, 292.

21. *OR*, vol. 11, pt. 2, pp. 789–90, 797; Burton, *Extraordinary Circumstances*, 245–46.

22. Browning, *Seven Days' Battles*, 118.

23. Browning, *The Seven Days' Battles*, 119.

24. Six of the sixteen batteries of the Artillery Reserve were temporarily attached to infantry commands.

25. Spruill and Spruill, *Echoes of Thunder*, 243–45; *OR*, vol. 11, pt. 2, pp. 238, 243, 252, 265.

26. Browning, *The Seven Days' Battles*, 109, 118.

27. The reserve is a force held back from the main or supporting attacks, and it is positioned so as to support or exploit the success of the main attack.

28. The main attack is designed to capture the enemy position or achieve the overall objective. It has the majority of troops and priority of supporting artillery fire.

29. The supporting attack(s) hold the enemy forces in position, cause premature or incorrect commitment of the enemy's reserve, and confuse the enemy as to which is the main attack.

30. Browning, *The Seven Days' Battles*, 118–20; Burton, *Extraordinary Circumstances*, 269.

31. *OR*, vol. 11, pt. 2, p. 666; Browning, *The Seven Days' Battles*, 119–20.

32. *OR*, vol. 11, pt. 2, pp. 666–67.

33. *OR*, vol. 11, pt. 2, pp. 666–67.

Chapter 4

1. Browning, *The Seven Days' Battles*, 130–31.

2. Browning, *The Seven Days' Battles*, 130–31.

3. Burton, *Extraordinary Circumstances*, 312.

4. Browning, *The Seven Days' Battles*, 133, 135–36; Burton, *Extraordinary Circumstances*, 314–16.

5. Browning, *The Seven Days' Battles*, 133, 135–36; Burton, *Extraordinary Circumstances*, 314–16.

6. D. H. Hill had five brigades, Whiting had two, Winder had four, Huger had four, Magruder had two, Jones had two, and McLaws had two.

7. *OR*, vol. 11, pt. 2, p. 677.

8. Spruill and Spruill, *Echoes of Thunder*, 215, 221.

9. Browning, *The Seven Days' Battles*, 139.

10. "Complete Sun and Moon Date for One Day."

11. Burton, *Extraordinary Circumstances*, 330.

12. Spruill and Spruill, *Echoes of Thunder*, 228; Burton, *Extraordinary Circumstances*, 332; William Allen, *The Army of Northern Virginia in 1862* (San Bernardino, CA: First Rate, 2015), npn.

13. Spruill and Spruill, *Echoes of Thunder*, 231; Burton, *Extraordinary Circumstances*, 343, 349; Allen, *The Army of Northern Virginia in 1862.*

14. Spruill and Spruill, *Echoes of Thunder*, 236; Burton, *Extraordinary Circumstances*, 343; Browning, *The Seven Days' Battles*, 147.

15. Browning, *The Seven Days' Battles*, 141–47; Brian K. Burton, *The Peninsula and Seven Days: A Battlefield Guide* (Lincoln: University of Nebraska Press, 2007), 112–13.

16. Total Seven Days casualties were 15,795 Union combatants and 20,204 Confederate combatants.

17. Sears, *To the Gates of Richmond*, 156, 195.

18. *OR*, vol. 11, pt. 52, pp. 165, 203, 275–76, 351, 404, 431.

19. Browning, *The Seven Days' Battles*, 150–51; Sears, *To the Gates of Richmond*, 338.

20. Browning, *The Seven Days' Battles*, 152; Sears, *To the Gates of Richmond*, 338.

21. Sears, *To the Gates of Richmond*, 339.

22. Sears, *To the Gates of Richmond*, 339.

23. Donald, *Lincoln*, 359–61.

24. Warner, *Generals in Blue*, 195–97; Boatner, *Civil War Dictionary*, 353, 367.

25. Thomas E. Griess, ed., *The American Civil War: The West Point Military History Series* (Wayne, NJ: Avery, 1987), 50; Nevins, *War for the Union*, 2:58–59; Dowdey, *Seven Days*, 70–71.

26. Lenoir Chambers, *Stonewall Jackson*, vol. 1, *The Legend and the Man to Valley V* (1959; repr., Wilmington, NC: Broadfoot, 1988), 471–72, 554; Steele, *American Campaigns*, 220.

27. Griess, *American Civil War*, 50.

28. Boatner, *The Civil War Dictionary*, 792; website: https://www.nps.gov /people/edwin-m-stanton.htm.

29. Matt Spruill III and Matt Spruill IV, *Summer Lightning: A Guide to the Second Battle of Manassas* (Knoxville: University of Tennessee Press, 2013), 2.

30. Warner, *Generals in Blue*, 376; John J. Hennessy, *Return to Bull Run: The Campaign and Battle of Second Manassas* (New York: Simon and Schuster, 1993), 4–5; *OR*, vol. 12, pt. 3, 435.

31. *OR*, vol. 12, pt. 3, p. 435; Cozzens, *General John Pope*, 75–76.

32. Stephen E. Ambrose, *Halleck: Lincoln's Chief of Staff* (Baton Rouge: Louisiana State University Press, 1962), 67; Sears, *To the Gates of Richmond*, 351–52.

33. William C. Davis, *Death in the Trenches: Grant at Petersburg* (Alexandria, VA: Time-Life Books, 1986), 2–3.

34. The Army of the Potomac and Army of Virginia had a combined strength of 130,000. George Constable, ed., *Lee Takes Command: From the Seven Days to Second Bull Run* (Alexandria, VA: Time-Life Books, 1986), 124.

35. Ambrose, *Halleck*, 66–69.

36. Browning, *The Seven Days' Battles*, 156.

Chapter 5

1. The Battle of Stones River was fought from December 31, 1862, to January 2, 1863. The majority of the fighting and casualties occurred on December 31, 1862.

Appendix I

1. James Longstreet, *From Manassas to Appomattox: Memoirs of the Civil War in America* (Secaucus, NJ: Blue and Gray), 121–22.

2. *OR*, vol. 11, pt. 2, pp. 498–99.

3. *OR*, vol. 11, pt. 2, pp. 834–35.

4. *OR*, vol. 11, pt. 2, pp. 384–85.

5. *OR*, vol. 11, pt. 2, p 841.

6. *OR*, vol. 11, pt. 2, p. 426.

7. *OR*, vol. 11, pt. 2, p. 899.

8. *OR*, vol. 11, pt. 2, pp. 647–48.

9. *OR*, vol. 11, pt. 2, pp. 223–26.

10. *OR*, vol. 11, pt. 2, pp. 624–26.

11. *OR*, vol. 11, pt. 2, p. 55.

12. *OR*, vol. 11, pt. 2, p. 627.

13. *OR*, vol. 11, pt. 2, 561.

14. *OR*, vol. 11, pt. 2, p. 55.

15. *OR*, vol. 11, pt. 2, p. 495.

16. *OR*, vol 11, pt. 2, p. 759.

17. *OR*, vol. 11, pt. 2, pp. 496–97.

18. *OR*, vol 11, pt. 2, p. 802.

19. *OR*, vol 11, pt. 2, pp. 668–71.

20. *OR*, vol 11, pt. 2, pp. 573–74.

21. *OR*, vol 11, pt. 2, pp. 627–29.

22. *OR*, vol. 11, pt. 2, pp. 229–30.

23. *OR*, vol 11, pt. 2, p. 260.

24. *OR*, vol 11, pt. 2, pp. 313–15.

25. *OR*, vol. 11, pt. 1, pp. 80–81.

BIBLIOGRAPHY

Allen, William. *The Army of Northern Virginia in 1862*. San Bernardino, CA: First Rate, 2015.

Ambrose, Stephen E. *Halleck: Lincoln's Chief of Staff*. Baton Rouge: Louisiana State University Press, 1962.

Bailey, Ronald H. *Forward to Richmond: McClellan's Peninsula Campaign*. Alexandria, VA: Time-Life Books, 1983.

Boatner, Mark, III. *The Civil War Dictionary*. New York: David McKay, 1959.

Browning, Judkin. *The Seven Days' Battles: The War Begins Anew*. Santa Barbara, CA: Praeger, 2012.

Burton, Brian K. *Extraordinary Circumstances: The Seven Days Battles*. Bloomington: Indiana University Press, 2001.

———. *The Peninsula and Seven Days: A Battlefield Guide*. Lincoln: University of Nebraska Press, 2007.

Chambers, Lenoir. *Stonewall Jackson*. Vol. 2, *Seven Days to the Last March*. 1959. Reprint. Wilmington, NC: Broadfoot, 1988.

"Complete Sun and Moon Date for One Day." US Naval Observatory Astronomical Applications Department website. http://aa.usno.navy .mil/index.php.

Connelly, Thomas Lawrence. *Army of the Heartland: The Army of Tennessee, 1861–1862*. Baton Rouge: Louisiana State University Press, 1967.

Constable, George, ed. *Lee Takes Command: From the Seven Days to Second Bull Run*. Alexandria, VA: Time-Life Books, 1986.

Cozzens, Peter. *General John Pope: A Life for the Nation*. Urbana: University of Illinois Press, 2000.

Davis, William C. *Death in the Trenches: Grant at Petersburg*. Alexandria, VA: Time-Life Books, 1986.

———. *First Blood: Fort Sumner to Bull Run*. Alexandria, VA: Time-Life Books, 1983.

———. *Jefferson Davis: The Man and His Hour*. New York, NY: Harper-Collins Publishers, 1991.

Donald, David Herbert. *Lincoln*. London: Jonathan Cape Random House, 1995.

Doughty, Robert A., and Charles F. Brower IV. *The West Point Atlas of American Wars, Volume I: 1689–1900*. Rev. and updated ed. New York: Henry Holt, 1995.

Dowdey, Clifford. *The Seven Days: The Emergence of Robert E. Lee*. 1964. Reprint. Wilmington, NC: Broadfoot, 1988.

Dowdey, Clifford, and Louis H. Manarin, eds. *The Wartime Papers of Robert E. Lee*. 1961. Reprint. New York: Da Capo.

Early, Jubal A. *General Jubal A. Early: Autobiographical Sketch and Narrative of the War between the States*. 1912. Reprint. Wilmington, NC: Broadfoot, 1989.

Freeman, Douglas S. *Lee's Lieutenants: A Study in Command*. Vol. 1, *Manassas to Malvern Hill*. New York: Charles Scribner's Sons, 1942.

Griess, Thomas E., ed. *The American Civil War: The West Point Military History Series*. Wayne: NJ: Avery, 1987.

Harsh, Joseph L. *Confederate Tide Rising: Robert E. Lee and the Making of Southern Strategy, 1861–1862*. Kent, OH: Kent State University Press, 1998.

Hennessy, John J. *Return to Bull Run: The Campaign and Battle of Second Manassas*. New York: Simon and Schuster, 1993.

Kegel, James A. *North with Lee and Jackson: The Lost Story of Gettysburg*. Mechanicsburg, PA: Stackpole Books, 1996.

Knight, James R. *The Battle of Pea Ridge: The Civil War Fight for the Ozarks*. Charleston, SC: History Press, 2012.

Lee, Robert E. *Lee's Dispatches: Unpublished Letters of Robert E. Lee to Jefferson Davis.* Edited by Douglas S. Freeman 1915. Reprint. Baton Rouge: Louisiana State University Press, 1994.

Long, Armistead L. *Memoirs of Robert E. Lee: His Military and Personal History.* 1886. Reprint. Secaucus, NJ: Blue and Gray, 1983.

Longacre, Edward G. *The Man behind the Guns: A Biography of General Henry J. Hunt, Commander of Artillery, Army of the Potomac.* South Brunswick, NJ: A. S. Barnes, 1977.

Longstreet, James. *From Manassas to Appomattox: Memoirs of the Civil War in America.* Secaucus, NJ: Blue and Gray.

Marshall, Charles. *An Aide de Camp of Robert E. Lee: Being the Papers of Colonel Charles Marshall.* Edited by Frederick Maurice. Boston: Little, Brown, 1927.

McClellan, George B. "The Peninsula Campaign." In *Battles and Leaders of the Civil War: Being for the Most Part Contributions by Union and Confederate Officers,* edited by Robert U. Johnson and Clarence C. Buel. 2:168, 1884. Reprint. Secaucus, NJ: Castle Books, 1982.

McPherson, James M. *Battle Cry of Freedom: The Civil War Era.* New York: Oxford University Press, 1988.

Miller, William F., comp. "The Grand Campaign: A Journal of Operations on the Peninsula, March 17–August 26, 1862." In *The Peninsula Campaign of 1862: Yorktown to the Seven Days,* edited by William J. Miller, 1: 30, 94, 183, 186, 189, 205, Campbell, CA: Savas-Woodbury, 1993.

————. "Logistics, Friction and McClellan's Strategy for the Peninsula Campaign" in *The Peninsula Campaign of 1862: Yorktown to the Seven Days,* ed. William J. Miller, 2:136, 160, Campbell, CA: Savas-Woodbury, 1993.

Nevins, Allan. *The War for the Union: War Becomes Revolution, 1862–1863.* New York: Charles Scribner's Sons, 1960.

Palfrey, John C. "The Siege of Yorktown." In *Papers of the Military Historical Society of Massachusetts.* 1:98 *Campaigns in Virginia, 1861–1862,* edited by Theodore F. Dwight. 1895. Reprint. Wilmington, NC: Broadfoot, 1989.

Porter, Fitz John. "Hanover Court House and Gaines Mill." In *Battles and Leaders of the Civil War: Being for the Most Part Contributions by Union and Confederate Officers,* edited by Robert U. Johnson and Clarence C. Buel. Vol. 2. 1884. Reprint. Secaucus, NJ: Castle Books, 1982.

Sauers, Richard A. "The Pennsylvania Reserves." In *The Peninsula Campaign of 1862: Yorktown to the Seven Days*, edited by William J. Miller, 1:30. Campbell, CA: Savas-Woodbury, 1993.

Sears, Stephen W. *Lincoln's Lieutenants: The High Command of the Army of the Potomac*. Boston: Houghton Mifflin Harcourt, 2017.

———. *To the Gates of Richmond: The Peninsula Campaign*. New York: Ticknor and Fields, 1992.

Smith, Timothy B. *Shiloh: Conquer or Perish*. Lawrence: University Press of Kansas, 2014.

Spruill, Matt, III, and Matt Spruill IV. *Decisions at Second Manassas: The Fourteen Critical Decisions That Defined the Battle*. Knoxville: University of Tennessee Press, 2018.

———. *Echoes of Thunder: A Guide to the Seven Days Battles*. Knoxville: University of Tennessee Press, 2006.

Steele, Matthew Forney. *American Campaigns*. Washington, DC: Byron S. Adams, 1909.

Swinton, William. *Campaigns of the Army of the Potomac*. Secaucus, NJ: Blue and Gray, 1988.

Tanner, Robert G. *Stonewall in the Valley: Thomas J. "Stonewall" Jackson's Shenandoah Valley Campaign, Spring 1862*. Mechanicsburg, PA: Stackpole Books, 1996.

US War Department. *The War of the Rebellion: A Compilation of the Official Records of the Union and Confederate Armies*. 128 vols. Washington, DC: US Government Printing Office, 1880–1901.

Warner, Ezra J. *Generals in Blue: Lives of the Union Commanders*. Baton Rouge: Louisiana State University Press, 1964.

———. *Generals in Gray: Lives of the Confederate Commanders*. Baton Rouge: Louisiana State University Press, 1959.

Webb, Alexander S. *The Peninsula: McClellan's Campaign of 1862*. 1881. Reprint. Wilmington, NC: Broadfoot, 1989.

Woodworth, Steven E. *Davis and Lee at War*. Lawrence: University Press of Kansas, 1995.

INDEX

Gaines' Farm, 125
Gaines' Mill, Battle of, 3, 96, 97; D. H.
    Hill's attack, 130; Union position 123
Garland, Samuel, Brig. Gen., CSA
    (Bde Cmdr, ANV), 130, 150; at
    Gaines' Mill, 130; Malvern Hill
    attack, 79
Gibson, William, Col., CSA (Cmdr
    48th GA Inf, ANV), 120
Glendale, Battle of, 3; Union positions,
    137–38
Glendale, VA, 98, 99
Glendale Crossroads, 52, 57, 137; as a
    choke point, 57, 59, 137
Glorieta Pass, battle of, 1
Gloucester Point, VA, 9
Gordon, John B., Col., CSA (Regt &
    Bde Cmdr, ANV), 151; Malvern
    Hill attack, 79, 151
Gordonsville, VA, 36, 86
Grant, Ulysses S., Brig. Gen. & Maj.
    Gen., USA (Army Cmdr), 1, 84,
    100
Grapevine Bridge, 57, 130, 131
Grapevine Road, 131
Gregg, Maxcy, Brig. Gen., CSA
    (Bde Cmdr, ANV), 109, 111; bri-
    gade of, 109
Griffin, Charles, Brig. Gen., USA
    (Bde Cmdr, AP), 126; at Gaines'
    Mill, 126; at Malvern Hill, 156
Grimes, Carey F., Capt., CSA (Cmdr
    Portsmouth Btry, ANV), 145;
    report of 145
Gustin, Richard, Capt., USA (Cmdr
    Co C, 12th PA Res, AP), 116

Half Sink, VA, 29, 36, 106
Halleck, Henry W., Maj. Gen., USA
    (General-in-Chief, U.S. Army),
    87; appointed general-in-chief, 84;
    biography of, 84; critical decision,
    89–91, 99–100; orders Army of the
    Potomac back to Washington, 89,

100, 158; visits Army of the Poto-
    mac, 89, 99, 158
Hampton, Wade, Brig. Gen., CSA
    (Bde Cmdr, ANV), 60, 136
Hardaway, R. A., Capt., CSA (Cmdr
    Hardaway's Btry, ANV), 135
Harpers Ferry, VA, 13, 14, 23
Harrison's Landing, 81, 87, 99, 157, 158;
    Confederate position, 128; Union
    position, 83, 158; Union retreat to, 83
Harrison's Landing Road, 158
Harvey, Elisha B., Col., USA (7th PA
    Res, AP), 116
Hazzard, George W., Capt. USA (Cmdr
    Btrys A & C, 4th US Arty, AP), 136
Heintzelman, Samuel P., Brig. Gen.,
    USA (Corps Cmdr, AP) 10, 153;
    corps of, 59; position on Malvern
    Hill, 74, 80
Herring Creek Road, 157
Hill, Ambrose P., Maj. Gen., CSA
    (Div Cmdr, ANV), 22, 26, 31, 37,
    96, 109, 120; attacks at Beaver
    Dam Creek, 38, 41, 113–14; attacks
    at Glendale, 70; biography of, 34;
    critical decision, 33–43, 96; crosses
    Meadow Bridge, 38; deploys at
    Beaver Dam Creek, 113; division of
    29, 34, 44, 45, 57, 63, 65, 99, 109
Hill, Daniel H., Maj. Gen., CSA (Div
    Cmdr,ANV), 22, 31; at Beaver
    Dam Creek, 41, at Gaines' Mill,
    128–31; at White Oak Swamp, 60,
    65, 133–34; at Yorktown, 11; crosses
    Chickahominy River, 41, 111, 119;
    deploys at Gaines' Mill, 130; divi-
    sion of, 26, 29, 34, 44, 57, 106, 111,
    Malvern Hill Attack, 79, 149–51
Hoke, William J., Col., CSA (Cmdr
    38th NC Inf, ANV), 118
Holmes, Theophilus, Maj. Gen., CSA
    (Div Cmdr, ANV), 67, 140; attacks
    Malvern Hill, 69–70; division of,
    29, 58, 65, 67, 98, 99

Taggert, John H., Col., USA (Cmdr
  12th PA Res, AP), 116; report of,
  116–17
Telegraph Road, 122
Tennessee River, 2, 100
Toombs, Robert, Brig. Gen., CSA
  (Bde Cmdr, ANV), 151
Trent House, 131
Tucker, John, Asst Sec of War, USA, 8
Turkey Creek, 150
Tyler, Robert O., Col., USA (Cmdr
  Arty Siege Train, AP), 154

Unit designations, xvi-xvii
Urbanna, VA, 7

Virginia Central Railroad, 3, 6, 86, 88,
  110
Virginia Peninsula (The Peninsula) 3,
  49, 50, 53, 94

Walnut Grove Baptist Church, 122
Warrick River, 10
Washington, DC, 89, 94; McDowell's
  corps to protect, 10, 13
Watt House Road, 123
Watt House, 123
Waynesboro, VA, 36
Weldon Railroad, 88
West House, 143, 148, 152
West Point, VA, 7, 9, 48
White House Landing, VA, 33, 48, 96;
  as a supply base, 26
White Oak Bridge, 131, 132; impor-
  tance of, 132
White Oak Road, 132
White Oak Swamp, 59, 61, 98, 132;
  terrain, 59
Whiting, William H. C., Brig. Gen.,
  CSA (Div Cmdr, ANV), approach
  to Malvern Hill, 74; division of, 25,
  26; sent to reinforce Jackson, 24,
  25, 29

Williamsburg, VA, 17
Williamsburg Road, 26, 29, 57, 132
Willis Church Road, 73, 74, 137, 148
Wilson's Creek, Battle of, 1
Winchester, VA, 23
Winder, Charles S., Brig. Gen.,
  CSA (Div Cmdr, ANV), 128, 151;
  approaches Malvern Hill, 74; at
  Gaines' Mill, 130
Wooding, George W., Capt., CSA
  (Cmdr Wooding's Btry, ANV), 135
Wright, Ambrose, Brig. Gen., CSA
  (Bde Cmdr, ANV), 145; ap-
  proaches Malvern Hill, 74; Mal-
  vern Hill attack, 79, 146

York River, 7, 9, 48
Yorktown, VA, 9, 94